DATE DUE			MAY 0 6
GAYLORD			PRINTED IN U.S.A.

God Laughs & Plays

* * *

God Laughs & Plays

◆ ◆ ◆

CHURCHLESS SERMONS
IN RESPONSE TO THE PREACHMENTS
OF THE FUNDAMENTALIST RIGHT

David James Duncan

THE
TRIAD
INSTITUTE

Great Barrington, Massachusetts

PUBLISHED BY TRIAD BOOKS
a division of Triad Institute, Inc.
P.O. Box 601, Great Barrington, MA 01230
info@triadinstitute.org
www.triadinstitute.org

ISBN-10: 0-9777170-0-3
ISBN-13: 978-0-9777170-0-2
LCCN 2006900545

Distribution by
Itasca Distribution Services
5120 Cedar Lake Road
Minneapolis, MN 55416
800-901-3480, (FAX) 763-398-0198

April 2006
First Edition
10 9 8 7 6 5 4 3 2 1

Cover Design by Kyle Hunter
Book Design by Wendy Holdman

Contents

* * * * * * * *

Triad Institute Foreword

One of the greatest challenges faced by people living in the twenty-first century is to find a form of citizenship that works productively, sustainably, peaceably, inspirationally, artfully, and justly in a time of tremendous change and uncertainty. A time when, as Thomas Friedman describes, communications technology, the liberalization of markets, and other aspects of globalization have "flattened" the world, while global warming, aquifer depletion, species mega-extinction, soil depletion, excessive consumption in the industrialized world, and poverty and overpopulation in the developing world portend a very different kind of flattening.

The increasing threat and reality of terrorism add even greater immediacy and urgency to the problem. Anti-enlightenment and intolerant fundamentalism, whether in religious or political form, whether international or domestic, has in recent years cast a long shadow over progressive efforts for peace, justice, and sustainability. In the United States, our leadership's responses to the threat of terror have led not only to a weakening of civil liberties at home and an increasing belligerence abroad, but also to a simplification and chastening of the moral terrain surrounding the question of values.

For many, the last national election turned on the issue

of "moral values." In principle, the primacy given to moral values by so many in the United States is a good thing. As the dominant influence in the world and as a beacon of democracy, Americans and American leadership need to evince moral clarity. The values that guide our actions here and abroad must be founded upon an honest inquiry into what constitutes our moral compass. It is also crucial to understand that the search for a moral values–based vision of America is a process that evolves over time and is open to new ideas, information, and challenges. A moral American democracy, according to the founders, was not based on one imposed interpretation of truth. The Revolutionary War was fought and the Constitution written to protect from that kind of demagoguery. As Garry Wills wrote in a post-election essay that bemoaned the apparent move toward fundamentalism in the United States, "America, the first real democracy in history, was a product of Enlightenment values—critical intelligence, tolerance, respect for evidence, a regard for the secular sciences." The current reality is a marked departure from this history.

The Triad Institute believes that an effective inquiry into moral values and leadership needs to be based simultaneously on faith *and* reason. To be concerned about the lives of the unborn but neglectful of the impact of mercury poisoning from power plants on those unborn, as well as young children and women of childbearing age, is not moral. To believe in the spread of freedom across the globe without engaging in a dialogue with other nations about the best ways of achieving that end is not moral. To care about "family values" and community without embracing a notion of inclusiveness, without regard to religious affiliation, sexual orientation, or racial makeup, is not moral.

To extol the virtues of democratic principles while undermining the right of free speech and a free press is not
moral. To declare that homeland security is a priority but
to willingly obscure or ignore the immense threat of global
warming is not moral.

The fact that many Americans base their voting patterns on such a flawed or simplistic understanding of moral
values has profound implications for the United States
and the rest of the world. In terms of foreign policy, the
past several years provide ample evidence that a mind-set
of polarities—"for us or against us," good or evil—that ex-
empts more nuanced and sensitive approaches undermines
peace and security, both at home and abroad. Domestically,
it highlights a failure of our educational system—of, among
other things, our ability to distinguish between the need for
cultivating, in John Dewey's words, a "spiritual democracy,"
and the need for maintaining a clear separation between
church and state.

There is an urgent need to counter the dominant
worldview through the advancement of an enlightened
understanding of the roles and responsibilities of national
citizenship, both within the United States and abroad. We
must neutralize the "fundamentalist drag" that is weighing
down our progress, as American citizens and as global humanity, toward a more just, peaceful, and sustainable place.

Finding a new vision of engaged and circumspect national citizenship is, therefore, paramount. We must seek
a far-reaching and just citizenship that helps us transcend
our all-too-human baser instinct of greed and the tempta-
tion toward the bald use of our accumulated power, not to
mention our vulnerability to wanton fearmongering and religious demagoguery. When we Americans step into the voting

booth, we are no longer acting on the basis of one-person, one-vote, but rather on behalf of innumerable others around the world, whose lives hinge on our choices.

Having been concerned for some time about the rise of evangelical fundamentalism in the executive, legislative, and judicial branches of American government, and the resulting deterioration of the separation between church and state, I proposed a book project to David James Duncan. Our last collaboration, in 2003, resulted in the book *Citizens Dissent: Security, Morality, and Leadership in an Age of Terror* by Mr. Duncan and Wendell Berry, which won the 2003 Intellectual Freedom Award from the American Library Association. Duncan agreed to my request, and the result is this collection of "churchless sermons."

This new book contains, among other things, a powerful and timely critique of the conflation of neoconservative politics and apocalyptic evangelical fundamentalism. Notably, Duncan undertakes this critique not as an armchair critic with little or no experience of that of which he speaks, nor does he approach his subject matter from a purely scholarly or secular perspective. Born into a family of evangelicals, Duncan left the church as a teenager and has spent much of the rest of his life as a devoted conservationist and student of world religions and Wisdom texts, thoroughly engaging with the world as a lover of words and of trout streams.

In his prose we encounter a sensibility balanced between experience and introspection, outrage and compassion, passion and aestheticism, the earthly and the divine—a balance that gives rise to a voice of resonating wisdom and refreshing sincerity. A similar duality permeates the book in other ways. *God Laughs & Plays* is as urgent as a tire blowout in heavy traffic, yet also as enduring, nuanced, and comforting as fine wine and well-made bread. How does one explain this?

It is not just because David James Duncan is one of our finest writers. It is also, for me, a matter of cosmology. We, the peoples of Earth, need a new cosmology that can effectively embrace both our innate thirst for deeper, often obscured and intuited meanings as well as the necessary rigors of our intellectual life. We need a cosmology that can feed our souls and our questions about the meaning of life and death, while embracing the realities of our biological and ecological selves. A cosmology that reconciles our intimations of immortality with the facts of cellular disintegration, of genetic mutation and variation. A cosmology whose language retains over time its suppleness, beauty, and mystery—understanding both the potential as well as the limitations of language—and, through these, offers a powerful bulwark against the literalists and demagogues who invariably gather like turkey buzzards to prey on our ignorance and mortal vulnerabilities.

We need a new cosmology that can deepen our attunement with the natural world, recognizing the world as both a biological and spiritual source of sustenance, and a topographical map of ourselves and otherness. A mediating vehicle between, as Barry Lopez writes, the internal and external landscapes. A cosmology that can affirm and strengthen our role as "triadic" citizens—of communities, nations, and the world—in the face of globalization and ecological deterioration. A cosmology that helps us effectively manage such immanences as global warming, the global economy, global poverty, and war.

In short, we need a new cosmology that can help us deal with the immense challenges of the twenty-first century.

David James Duncan gives us a glimpse of what that cosmology might look like: a vision that is at once transcendent, beautiful, hopeful, and fierce. It is the vision of an activist sage. A sage ecologist. An ecological mystic.

Laurie Lane-Zucker, President
Triad Institute

* * * * * * * *

Bush Administration Sacks Narnia
Author's Preface

*The question before the human race is, whether the God
of nature shall govern the world by his own laws, or
whether priests and kings shall rule it by fictitious miracles.*

JOHN ADAMS TO THOMAS JEFFERSON, 1815

I was born a chosen person, though this state of affairs was
not of my choosing. My mother, grandmother, and great-
grandmother were staunch Seventh-day Adventists—an
Apocalypse-preaching, Saturday-worshiping fundamentalist sect that arose in the mid-nineteenth century. Our
faith's founder prophesied Jesus's Second Coming and "the
Rapture" in the 1840s. When both failed to occur, he instead
started the church into which the matriarchs of my family
were later born. These strong women gave their offspring
no choice but to attend the same churches and share their
faith, so attend and share we did. My father and grandfather,
however, did not go to church, and none of my friends at
public school were SDAs either. I, in other words, was
"saved"—no plagues of boils and frogs or eternal hellfire for
me—whereas my father, grandfather, and school friends
were, according to our preachers, impending toast.

Sound suspicious to you? It sure did to me. Intense spiritual feelings were frequent visitors during my boyhood, but they did not come from churchgoing or from bargaining with God through prayer. The connection I felt to the Creator came, unmediated, from Creation itself. The spontaneous gratitude I felt for birds and birdsong, tree-covered or snowcapped mountains, rivers and their trout, moon and starlight, summer winds on wilderness lakes, the same lakes silenced by winter snows, spring resurrections after autumn's mass deaths—the intimacy, intricacy, and interwovenness of these things—became the spiritual instructors of my boyhood. In even the smallest suburban wilds I felt linked to powers and mysteries I could sincerely imagine calling the Presence of God.

In fifteen years of churchgoing I did not once feel this same sense of Presence. What I felt instead was a lot of heavily agenda-ed, fear-based information being shoved at me by men on the church payroll. Though these men claimed to speak for God, I was never convinced. So on the day I was granted the option of what our preachers called "leaving the faith," I did leave—and increased my faith by so doing. Following intuition and love with all the sincerity and attentiveness I could muster, I consciously chose a life spent in the company of rivers, wilderness, Wisdom literature, like-minded friends, and quiet contemplation. And as it's turned out, this life—though dirt-poor in church pews—has enriched me with a sense of the holy, and left me far more grateful than I'll ever be able to say.

Three decades of intimacy with some of the world's greatest Wisdom texts and some of the West's most beautiful rivers led me to assume I'd escaped the orbit of organized religion. Then came a night in Medford, Oregon. Having given a literary reading to a warm, sometimes raucous, not-at-all-churchlike crowd, I was walking to the car afterward when one of the most astute men I know—my good friend Sam Alvord—clapped me on the back and amiably remarked, "I enjoy your evangelism."

The last word in Sam's sentence flabbergasted me. *Evangelism?* I was a storyteller, not one of those dang proselytizers! The evangelists I'd known since childhood thought the supposed "inerrancy of the Bible" magically neutralized their own flaming errancy and gave them an apostolic right to judge humanity and bilk it at the same time. The evangelists I'd known proclaimed themselves saved, the rest of us damned, and swore that only by shouting "*John 3:16! John 3:16!*" at others, as if selling Redemption Peanuts at a ballgame, could we avoid an Eternal State of Ouch. Evangelists, as I saw 'em, were a self-enlisted army of Cousin Sydneys from Mark Twain's *Tom Sawyer*, preaching a tattletale religiosity that boiled down to the cry: *If you don't believe what the Bible and me say, and pay me for saying it, I'm gonna tell God on you and you're gonna get in Big Trouble!*

Then clear-eyed, honest Sam tells me, "I enjoy your evangelism"?

Shit O. Deer.

My first response to Sam's remark was to repress the living bejeezus out of it. Ten years passed before I dared look up the "e-word" in *The Oxford English Dictionary*. What I finally found there was, well . . . I guess the word pretty much has to be: *damning*. Though the range of meanings surrounding the root word "evangel" is vast, a whole raft of definitions tied my public readings, literary writings, and me to Sam's characterization. Insofar as I believe Jesus is the bee's knees, and insofar as I speak words that could be seen as spreading the spiritual intent of the gospels, I must confess, with "fear and trembling," that I am (gulp!) *evangelical.*

Having damned myself in what we might call "anti-evangelical circles," I'd like to qualify that damnation.

Religious laws, in all the major traditions, have both a letter and a spirit. As I understand the words and example of Jesus, the spirit of a law is all-important, whereas the letter, while useful in conjunction with spirit, becomes lifeless and deadly without it. In accord with this distinction, a yearning to worship on wilderness ridges or beside rivers, rather than in churches, could legitimately be called evangelical. Jesus Himself began His mission after forty days and nights in wilderness. According to the same letter-vs.-spirit distinction, the law-heavy literalism of many so-called evangelicals is not evangelical at all: "evangel" means "the gospels"; the essence of the gospels is Jesus; and literalism is (literally!) not something that Jesus personified or taught.

Christ's words also suggest to me that one needn't be a Christian for the word "evangelical" to apply: if your words or deeds harmonize with the example of Jesus, you are evangelical in spirit whether you claim to be or not. When the non-Christian Ambrose Bierce, for instance, wrote, "War is the means by which Americans learn geography," there was acid dripping almost visibly from his pen. His words, however, are aimed at the same antiwar end as the gospel statements "Love thine enemies" and "Love thy neighbor as thyself." And *Blessed are the peacemakers.*" Bierce's wit is in this sense evangelical whether he likes it or not.

In reclaiming a word like "evangelical" from those who think they own it, we risk making some people mad. But there are reasons to take this risk. Fundamentalist Christians, Muslims, Hindus, and Jews are armed, so they each believe, with the One True Book. But they are four different books, and the four faiths are also each armed with nuclear weapons. No form of fundamentalism from the Ayatollahs' to John Paul II's can defuse this fatal impasse, because every fundamentalism believes it owns the One Book, One God, and sole faith. At the same time, no secular philosophy addresses the fact that we're born alone and die alone, and naturally seek the solace of divine truth amid our mortal suffering. Though the faith traditions offer this solace, I would argue that they are able to do so only quietly, and only humbly—and the recent fusion of fundamentalism and politics is destroying this quiet humility. This is why I feel the great religious traditions stand in need not of a secular turning away, but of a compassion rebellion against the "certainties" of cocksure zealots claiming to own each tradition. The fundamentalists of every faith remain blind to the truth that "the sigh within the prayer is the same in the heart of the Christian, the Muhammadan, and the Jew." I have seen this unity with my eyes, heard it with my ears, felt it with all my being. Let those who haven't grumble, if they so choose. The world's major faiths are not identical, but they are alike enough in ultimate aim that those striving to love, emulate, and honor Jesus, Muhammad, Rama, Shakyamuni, and Abraham have, in many times and places, proven themselves able to live side by side in peace. I consider it *evangelical* and *Christian*, in the gospel-born sense of these words, to serve this fragile peace.

The appropriation of Christian terminology by the American political faction known as neoconservative has resulted in a brand of fundamentalist I'm tempted to call "avengeli-cal," but in the interests of diplomacy will simply call "right-wing." The fusion of religiosity and right-wing politics has created a mood of vehemence in millions. It has changed America's leadership, altered our collective identity in the eyes of the world, and destroyed our civility at home. Opponents of the right-wing/fundamentalist conflation are now demonized not just as "traitors to America" but as enemies of a new kind of Americanized God. Even those who seek to love and steward the earth are now sometimes demonized by those who've decided it's time for God's creation to be destroyed.

Where, I recently found myself wondering, *have I seen something like this before?*

And it hit me: *The Chronicles of Narnia.*

In this children's fantasy series by C. S. Lewis, the populace of the Land of Narnia consists of talking animals, and their Christ figure is embodied by a magnificent lion named Aslan. When he incarnates in Narnia this christic lion chooses, despite his great predatory power, to turn himself over to his enemies. These enemies then kill him—slowly, unmercifully, and graphically, though the scene is intended for children—on a stone table. The result is heartbreak for Aslan's devotees, soon followed by a transformative wonder: it turns out the blood of the Lion, once shed, possesses a spiritual power far greater than the strength, teeth, and claws of any animal. It turns out the christic cannot be killed. Aslan rises from the dead in a physical but also spiritual body capable of communing with the hearts of all Narnians who believe in him. And the land is transformed: the Lion's self-sacrifice inspires unselfishness, kindness to neighbors, love of homeland, heroic deeds, and beneficence for centuries to come.

So far so good. In the climactic volume of the series, however, Narnia falls into unprecedented trouble when a power-hungry ape, named Shift, hits on the idea of dressing a witless donkey, named Puzzle, in an ordinary lion's skin, then publically proclaiming the donkey to be the Christ-Lion. Not surprisingly, the ape's pronouncements via the gullible donkey serve little but the ape's selfish interests: "[We'll] make Narnia a country worth living in," he says. "There'll be oranges and bananas pouring in . . ." (his favorites) "and roads and big cities and schools and offices and whips and muzzles and saddles and cages and kennels and prisons and—Oh, everything."

For a while Shift and Puzzle rule in this manner and nothing much worse than confusion comes of it. Soon, though, the ape and donkey are overwhelmed by ruthless men from outside Narnia and become their helpless pawns. These men use the faux Christ-Lion's appeal to sculpt policies that soon put the talking animals of Narnia to work plundering their own land and homes to build Shift's "roads, whips, muzzles, and prisons," to the benefit of no one but the outsiders.

As Narnia is laid waste, the talking animals divide into two camps: Loyalists and Rebels. When the fake Aslan's pronouncements grow antithetical to freedom and deadly to Narnians, the Loyalists, though terribly confused, continue to hold their spiritual king in such high regard that they carry out even the most senseless and ruthless of "His" commands. The Rebels, on the other hand, judge Aslan afresh by the cruelty of the recent edicts, decide they must have been wrong to worship Him in the first place, and rebel against His rule. The friction that results is divisive and tragic for both sides.

I agree with C. S. Lewis that loyalty to an image of

Aslan or of Jesus is an act of faith, and that faith is moving.
I also agree with Lewis that a counterfeit lion is the bitter-
est enemy of those who would follow the True Lion. The
respective iron, crimson, and flaming crosses of the Nazi
party, Spanish Inquisition, and Ku Klux Klan prove that
images of Jesus can stand for all kinds of things besides
love of Jesus. A growing number of people of faith—a great
many Christians included—believe that Americans are currently being asked to worship a kind of donkey in christic
disguise. Examples of the deception are numerous. I'll limit
myself to two that came to my attention through the writings of the evangelical Christian Jim Wallis.

On the first anniversary of the destruction of the World
Trade Center, President Bush gave a speech in New York in
which he said that the *"ideal of America is the hope of all mankind."* Six billion people on earth are not Americans; to call
America their hope is, to put it mildly, hubristic. What's more,
anyone who places their hope not in nations but in God is
obligated by their faith to find Bush's statement untrue. But
the president's speechwriters ratcheted the rhetoric up even
further. After calling America the world's hope, Bush added,
*"That hope still lights our way. And the light shines in the dark-
ness. And the darkness has not overcome it."* As Wallis points
out in "Dangerous Religion" (*Mississippi Review*, Vol. 10,
No. 1), these sentences are lifted straight from the gospel of
John, wherein they refer not to America or any nation, but
to the Word of God and the light of Christ.

"You look wonderful," Shift the ape tells Puzzle the donkey the first time he dresses him in the lion's skin. "If anyone
saw you now they'd think you were Aslan, the Great Lion
himself."

"That would be dreadful," the donkey replies.

"No it wouldn't!" the ape counters. "Everyone would do

whatever you told them. . . . Think of the good we could do!
You'd have me to advise you, you know. I'd think of sensible
orders for you to give. And everyone would have to obey us."

Second example of the Bush team playing Shift's game:
in his 2003 State of the Union address the president said
that there is "power, wonder-working power in the good-
ness and idealism and faith of the American people"—
words stolen from a hymn that in fact says there is "power,
wonder-working power *in the blood of the Lamb*" (my em-
phasis). This thievery is breathtaking, and leaves me wondering what Bush's speechwriters might steal next. John 1:1
perhaps? "*In the beginning was America, and America was
with God, and America was God.*"

"The real theological problem in America today," writes
Wallis, is "the nationalist religion . . . that confuses the identity of the nation with the church, and God's purposes with
the mission of American empire. America's foreign policy
is more than pre-emptive, it is theologically presumptuous;
not only unilateral, but dangerously messianic; not just ar-
rogant, but . . . blasphemous."

I would add the Bush administration's notion of stewardship to Wallis's list of blasphemies. To describe the current
war on nature as "stewardship" is to forsake the teachings
of the Bible. In Genesis, men and women are made in the
image of the God who just created and blessed all creatures
and their ability to multiply, Adam is placed in Eden merely
"to dress it and keep it," and Noah takes enormous pains
to preserve Earth's God-given biological diversity from the
God-sent Flood. In Exodus, the Sabbath rest is given to
animals as well as humans. In Leviticus, humans are told
by God to tend the land carefully and not treat it as a possession, because, "the land is mine, and you are but aliens

who have become my tenants." In the Psalms, "The Earth is the Lord's, and the fullness thereof." Then in the gospels we meet, in Jesus, a leader who refuses political power and defines dominion as "Thy will be done, on earth as it is in heaven"—a king of kings whose life is characterized throughout by sensitivity to the meek, the weak, the poor, the voiceless, field lilies, the fowls of the air, and all other forms of life.

American fundamentalists, despite avowed love for this same Jesus, predominately support a Bush administration that has worked to weaken the Clear Air and Clean Water Acts and gut the Endangered Species and Environmental Policy Acts. This administration has stopped fining air and water polluters, dropped all suits against coal-fired power, weakened limits on pollutants that destroy ozone, stopped citizen review of logging proposals in the people's own forests, and shown a near-total lack of support for clean energy, biofuels, energy conservation, mass transit, high-speed trains, and higher-mileage cars at the same time it has promised to blast, drill, and pipe the Arctic Wildlife sanctuary. I wish that none of this were so. I wish that ecosystem failures, extinctions, melting polar ice caps, ever-more-powerful hurricanes, and man-created cancers were not raining down upon us as I write. But since they are, I must ask in the name of every biblical steward from Adam to Jesus: how Christian is the cunning of speechwriters who place words meant to praise God, or Christ's spilled blood, in the mouth of a man who instead uses them to exalt an empire born of the destruction of America's own biological diversity and health?

The president calls himself "a good steward of the land," but followers of Jesus are instructed to judge leaders not by their words but "by their fruits." One of hundreds of

Bush administration stewardship fruits has been the increase in the amount of mercury in the air and waters of the same America we ask God to bless. The Bush team dubbed this legislation the "Clean Skies Initiative." Shift the ape couldn't have come up with a more cynical name. To call mercury "clean" is what schoolchildren who have not been "Left Behind" are correctly taught to call a lie. One in six American women already have so much mercury in their reproductive organs that their babies are at risk of being born blind, mentally retarded, autistic, or diseased. The fish in thousands of American lakes and streams are inedible due to mercury. We possess sustainable energy sources that would rid our skies, water, and soil of this poison. That the Bush administration works to subvert or delay the deployment of this technology is frustrating, but its removal of the New Source Rule from the Clean Air Act moved beyond frustrating. This rule caused deadly particulate matter to be removed from the coal-burning industry's emissions. American children and pregnant women now unavoidably eat and breathe Bush-released mercury-laden materials. The elimination of the New Source rule, according to the Environmental Protection Agency's own website, results in 18,000 dead Americans a year—six times the number killed in the World Trade Center attack.

To call this "Clean Skies" is neither stewardship nor Christianity: it is Shift-the-ape-like duplicity meant to enrich a wealthy few at the fatal expense of many.

What if Shift told Puzzle the donkey not to worry about stuff like mercury poisoning because of an impending global miracle called "the Rapture"? What if the ape promised the donkey that all good Narnians would be whisked away to heaven before the effects of their rape of Narnia took hold, and that they'd rest in the bliss of Aslan's embrace, watching from Above, as Narnia was visited by plagues culminating in its destruction?

My response would be: Déjà vu, Shift. Welcome to America circa 2006, America circa the 1840s, Italy circa 1500, and all of Europe at the time of Luther, the time of the Black Death, and in every other spasmodic period in its history.

Having been raised in a faith founded by a "prophet" who predicted Jesus's Second Coming in 1844, I have trouble with Tim LaHaye's and Jerry Falwell's "Rapture Index" and Second Coming scenarios. When the Lord didn't show in 1844, or the next year either, our SDA patriarch shrugged, started the church that eventually became the One True Sect into which I was born, and *still* kept preaching an Apocalypse that excluded everyone but his own minuscule faith community. God save me from yet another such chosenness. It appalled me as a boy to listen to "our" preachers exult as they predicted their own blissful rising up from Earth just in time to watch those who did not share the SDA faith suffer a skein of plagues, then fall into hell. What kind of "bliss" or "love" seeks the destruction and eternal suffering of all with whom the lover disagrees?

There is no doubt that good-hearted people yearn for the Second Coming. Such yearning, however, can also be judged by its fruits. Sandro Botticelli was a Florentine painter who believed the Second Coming would occur in 1500. Though his prophecy didn't amount to beans, the paintings it inspired were beautiful. We can perhaps trust a yearning that leads to self-giving, justice, or beauty. But yearning that leads to support of legislation like the Clean Skies Initiative, even if based on a desire for Jesus's return, is antithetical to everything Jesus personified, said, and did. It's hard to believe this is the way to please Him. To separate the word "Christian" from the person, teachings, and example of Jesus is to render it meaningless. The recent fusion of neocon politics and fundamentalism has manufactured this meaninglessness as surely as has any form of "secularism," with the added hypocrisy of invoking Christ's name while so doing.

Evangelism as embodied by Jesus does not remotely suggest the close-minded zeal of proselytizers claiming that only their interpretation of scripture prevents eternal punishments and pays eternal rewards: it implies, on the contrary, the kind of all-embracing love evident in Mother Teresa's prayer, "*May God break my heart so completely that the whole world falls in.*" Not just her fellow nuns, Catholics, Calcuttans, potential converts. *The whole world.*

It gives me pause to realize that, were such a prayer said by me and answered by God, I would afterward possess a heart so open that even hate-driven zealots would fall inside. There is a self-righteous knot in me that finds zealotry so repugnant it wants to sit on the sidelines with the like-minded, plaster my car with bumper stickers that say MEAN PEOPLE SUCK and NO BILLIONAIRE LEFT BEHIND and WHO WOULD JESUS BOMB?, and leave it at that. But I can't. My sense of this life as pure gift—my sense of a grace operative in this world despite, and even *amid*, its hurts and terrors—propels me to allow life to open my heart still wider, even if this openness comes by breaking. For I have seen the whole world fall into a few hearts, and nothing has ever struck me as more beautiful.

The whole world, for example, seemed to fall into the heart of Mahatma Gandhi, not only on the day he said, "*I am a Christian, I am a Hindu, I am a Muslim, I am a Jew,*" but on the day he proved the depth of his declaration when, after receiving two fatal bullets from a fundamentalist zealot, he blessed that zealot with a *namasté* before dying. For the fundamentalists of each tradition he names, Gandhi's fourfold profession of faith is three-fourths heresy. But it is also a statement that makes livable sense of Jesus's "love thy neighbor as thyself" and, for me personally, a description of spiritual terrain in which I yearn to take up residence. If, because of this yearning, these pages are found offensive by some, how can I not feel honored by that very offense?

Christians revere Jesus, Muslims *Allah*, Jews *YHWH*, "He who causes to be," and Hindus *Brahman*, "the Big," who speaks the Beginning/Middle/End word, *AUM*. This variety creates differences. Yet each faith holds that its holy Names cannot be properly said lest we first garb ourselves in utmost humility and surround our naming with silence. And each faith calls humanity to love, service, and stewardship. All acts of love, service, and stewardship, we might therefore contend, are holy.

To put the call in Christian terms: it is *this* world, not the next, that God loved so much that He bequeathed it His Son. In response to the Armageddon fantasies of His day, the Son said, "*The kingdom of God cometh not with observation. . . . For behold, the kingdom of God is within you.*"

This is an occasional book. It was put together at the request of Mr. Laurie Lane-Zucker of the Triad Institute, in response to a politically loaded derailment of American Christianity that Laurie and Triad see as one of the crises of our time. The book consists of what I call "churchless sermons" in the form of public talks, conversations, or essays written or said in boundless, though closeted (Matthew 6:6!), admiration of a Jesus whose life moves me to repudiate much of the preaching being done in His name today. Some of what follows are formal essays. Some is spontaneous talk lifted from interviews. Most of these words, though, were first spoken to audiences gathered for a particular occasion (say, the Feast Day of St. Francis) or in response to a particular crisis (say, the annihilation of wild salmon, or sanctioned elimination of medicine in Iraq). My public talks tend to begin redundantly, often by referring to the time, place, and occasion. I could edit out this repetitiousness and make the talks "more literary," but to do so feels somehow wrong. The preachers I most admire don't smooth their rough edges. I love the multitudinous exclamation points peppering the mystical homilies of Meister Eckhart, the hoot owl laughter invading the talks of Archbishop Desmond Tutu, and the English divine Sydny Smith's characterization of his own sermons as being "long and vigorous, like the penis of a jackass."

My life as a pew-poor, river-rich itinerant storyteller, writing teacher, and churchless preacher has been conducted in mostly playful, but occasionally heartbroken, response to the conservation and cultural crises of my time. References to time, place, and crisis will therefore be left in plain sight. My hope is that, despite a few heartbreaks, these words will convey a hint of my ongoing delight in and immense gratitude for this life, this time, this place.

David James Duncan
Western Montana, winter 2006

God Laughs & Plays

✦ ✦ ✦

Why is it only Christians who cannot see the nonviolence of Jesus?

MAHATMA GANDHI

◆

Children, how hard is it for them that trust in riches to enter into the kingdom of God!

JESUS

◆

Man desires a world where good and evil can be clearly distinguished, for he has an innate and irrepressible desire to judge before he understands.

MILAN KUNDERA

◆

If Christianity cannot recover its mystical tradition, and teach it, it should simply fold up and go out of business.

BEDE GRIFFITHS

◆

The Christian of the coming century will be a mystic or he will not be.

KARL RAHNER
(in the last century)

◆

*The way I see it, a mystic takes a peek at God
and then does her best to show the rest of us what
she saw. She'll use image-language, not discourse.
Giving an image is the giving of gold, the biggest
thing she's got. . . . Hurling and wielding the best
stuff she can imagine, insisting on an unmediated
Way of Wakefulness, . . . she agrees to the quiet
morning hour in front of God in exchange for a
bit of revelation. She doesn't ditch tradition as
much as take it for its word and peer inside its
cavernous shell. There must still be something
worth saying, worth pointing to.*

JESSIE HARRIMAN

✦

*Truly! Truly! By God! By God! Be as sure of
it as you are that God lives: at the least good
deed done here in this world, the least bit of
good will, the least good desire, all the saints in
heaven and on earth rejoice, and together with
the angels their joy is such that all the joy in this
world can't be compared. But the joy of them
all together amounts to as little as a bean when
compared to the joy of God over good deeds.
For truly, God laughs and plays.*

MEISTER ECKHART

Wonder; Yogi; Gladly

Several Decembers ago I was invited, in my capacity as a novelist and freelance writing teacher, to a little Christian college extension built out of a converted logging camp in tiny Lincoln, Oregon. I'm not too big on Christianizing efforts, generally speaking, but if there is anything on earth I like seeing converted it's logging camps. I was glad to be in Lincoln, happy with the look of my forty students, glad for the whole gig—until the students collectively informed me, the first night, that what they wanted me to talk about in the morning was my "personal faith" and "experiences as a churchgoer."

This simple request presented three immediate and considerable problems.

First problem: the phrase "personal faith" is impossibly paradoxical. As soon as you talk publicly about personal life, personal finances, personal anything, it's no longer personal.

Second problem: for the past thirty-five years I haven't had any "experiences as a churchgoer." Though I was raised, like most of my audience, in one of those fundamentalist denominations the preachers call a "fold," from the day I heard a trout stream give a sermon I began to hear the word "fold" as the move one makes in poker when one's cards aren't worth a damn. I've lived a faith life rich in rivers, poor in church services, and deep in gratitude ever since.

Third problem: like Mahatma Gandhi famously and countless less famous others, I revere Jesus and the gospels, but also Rama, Krishna, Buddha, Muhammad, Abraham, and other Prophets. The Christian turf is said by many to exclude this kind of "extra-Christianness," but my heart is by nature inclusive, and I seek to live by heart. I therefore conduct my faith life, wholeheartedly, outside the exclusive definition, and honestly don't know—or much care, so long as the preceding Prophets know I adore them—whether I'm "a Christian" or not.

So then. Bivouacked among the young Christians, with a couple of midnight hours to prepare my remarks on personal faith and personal churchgoing in order to earn my personal honorarium, I grew disturbingly cognizant, for the first time in my life, of a slight vocational resemblance between me and Pat Robertson. I sat down with a yellow legal pad and began dutifully jotting faith notes. But almost the first words I jotted were: "Isn't faith worth having precisely to the degree that it is *not* personal? The degree to which it's a gift rather than an invention? The degree to which it grasps us, rather than us grasping it?" With these three questions I gave myself an instant splitting headache, for now it appeared that I must speak of a brand of faith in which I have no faith. Because of the accursed wholesomeness on this nice little campus, there wasn't even any booze available to fuel the note jotting or ease the ache.

As the hour grew late I considered begging the religious side of the question and talking about things in which I really *do* place faith: Winston flyrods; Stihl chain saws; Coleman Barks's Rumi translations; Carl Ernst's Sufi scholarship;

A. K. Coomaraswamy's metaphysics; Toyota pickups; Walla Walla red wines; aged sharp Tillamook cheese; Roland keyboards; Blue Lion dulcimers. If I made my faith talk into a virtual cable shopping channel, I figured the televangelical-type Christians would feel right at home.

Trouble was, these kids didn't look so televangelical. They looked sharp as a bunch of damned tacks, actually. To be asked a sincere question is an honor. To answer such a question dishonestly is dishonorable. It took some desperate midnight doing, but after ouijaing around in my interior I managed to cull three words in which I had gained faith as a childhood churchgoer—words in which, all these years later, I still have faith.

The three words were "wonder," "Yogi," and "gladly." And my remarks to the young Christians the next morning follow. But first I want to say how stunned I was, and how grateful I remain, for the attentiveness, kindness, and openheartedness with which those forty or so students greeted a stranger's admittedly unorthodox thoughts.

Word #1. WONDER

My earliest conception of the meaning of this word was a feeling that would come over me, as a little kid, when I pictured the shepherds on the night hills above Bethlehem. Even when these shepherds were made of illuminated plastic, standing around in Christmas dioramas on my neighbor's lawn, their slack-jawed expressions of wonder appealed to me. Years later, having become literate enough to read a Bible, I learned that the shepherds were also "sore afraid." But—a personal prejudice—I didn't believe in their sore afraidness. I believed the star in the East smote them with sheer wonder, and my experience of wonder is that, once it smites you, you're smitten by wonder alone. Fear can't penetrate till wonder subsides.

Wonder is my second favorite condition to be in, after love—and I sometimes wonder whether there's even a difference: maybe love is just wonder aimed at a beloved. Wonder is like grace, in that it's not a condition we grasp: wonder grasps us. We do have the freedom to elude wonder's grasp. We have the freedom to do all sorts of stupid things. By deploying cynicism, rationalism, fear, arrogance, judgmentalism, we can evade wonder nonstop, all our lives. I'm not too fond of that gnarly old word, *sin*, but the deliberate evasion of wonder does bring it to mind. It may not be biblically sinful to evade wonder. But it is artistically and spiritually sinful.

Like grace, wonder defies rational analysis. Discursive thought can bring nothing to an object of wonder. Thought at best just circumambulates the object, the way a devout pilgrim circles Golgotha, the Bo Tree, Wounded Knee, the Kaabah. Wonder is not an obligatory element in the search for truth. We can seek truth without wonder's assistance— but seek is all we can do: there will be no finding. Until wonder descends, unlocks us, turns us slack-jawed as a plastic shepherd, truth is unable to enter. Wonder may be the aura of truth, the halo of it. Or something even closer. Wonder may be the caress of truth, touching our very skin.

Philosophically speaking, wonder is crucial to finding knowledge yet has everything to do with ignorance. Only an admission of ignorance can open us to fresh knowing. Wonder is the experience of that admission: wonder is unknowing, experienced as pleasure. Wonder is a period at the end of a statement we've long taken for granted, suddenly looking up and seeing the sinuous curve of a tall black hat on its head, and realizing it was a question mark all along.

As a facial expression, wonder is the letter O our eyes and mouths make when the state itself descends. O: God's middle initial. O: because wonder Opens us. O(ld) becoming new. Wonder is anything taken for granted—the old neighborhood, old job, old buddy, old spouse—suddenly filling with mystery. Wonder is anything closed, suddenly opening: anything at all opening—which includes Pandora's box, and brings me to the dark side of wonder. Grateful as I am for this condition, wonder, like everything on earth, has a dark side. Heartbreak, grief, and suffering rip openings in us through which the dark kind of wonder pours. I have so far found it impossible to be spontaneously grateful for these openings. But when, after struggle, I've been able to turn a corner and at least *accept* the openings, dark wonder has helped me endure the heartbreak, the suffering, the grief.

I believe it is wonder, even more than fidelity, that keeps marriages alive. I believe it is wonder, more than courage, that conquers fear of death. I believe it is wonder, not D.A.R.E. bumper stickers, that keeps kids off drugs. I believe, speaking of old bumper stickers, that it is wonder, even more than me, that I want to "HUG MY KIDS YET TODAY," because wonder can keep on hugging them long after I'm gone.

Word #2.   YOGI

Language can be a tool of oppression. It can be a tool of exquisite expression. And it can be some weird combination of both. Consider the utterances of New York Yankee legend Yogi Berra.

When told that the newly elected mayor of Dublin was a Jew, Yogi rasped, "Only in America!"

When his lifelong friend, Mickey Mantle, had died, Yogi

was offended, he said, "'cause the Mick an' me always promised to attend each other's funerals."

Of Yankee Stadium, Yogi said, "It gets late early there."

To the players he was coaching, Yogi said: "All right you guys, pair up in threes."

Yogi said: "Nobody goes there anymore. It's too crowded."

He said: "I really didn't say everything I said."

He said: "The future just idn't what it used to be."

Said: "When you come to a fork in the road, take it."

Said: "If you can't copy 'em, don't imitate 'em."

Each of these sentences is wonderfully right in its wrongness, bending the common usage the way a good blues guitarist bends his strings. Yogi Berra is living proof that it's possible to celebrate our linguistic pratfalls. I don't know how he does it, but I know this: he doesn't do it on purpose. As the Yog tries to grasp something else entirely, wonderful sentences grasp him. And being grasped—by wonder, by blunders, by the moment, by the day—being seized by things, rather than trying to do all the seizing myself: this is something I have huge faith in. I trust what comes to me, what befalls me, more than I trust what I aim at or seize for myself. Look what became of Rome, a nation led by Seizers.

As a child I was taught by certain pious adults that what is funny or pleasurable, and what is holy, are two separate categories. When I was twelve years old, for instance, I was thrown out of church one weekday evening by a Seventh-day Adventist man veiny with rage, for sneaking into the main sanctuary and playing, for a few friends, the Ramsey Lewis version of "Hang On Sloopy" on the church's big grand piano.

"This is *God's House!*" the man roared in my face.

"That was Ramsey Lewis's music," I peeped in reply.

"Get out!" he bellowed, *seizing* me by the scruff of my blazer.

"Okay," I said, and left.

It was a gorgeous piano, that one in the church: a big black Baldwin grand. The music I'd been playing was the first rhythm and blues my scrawny white fingers had ever mastered. The entire church building, except for my friends, our Bible teacher, and one unsuspected landmine of a man, had been empty. In Buddhism, "Vast Emptiness" (cf. Bodhidharma) is the spiritual goal. I don't know who Sloopy is in Buddhism, but in the song he's the protagonist. *"Hang on Sloopy, Sloopy hang on!"* the song tells him again and again. Hang on to what? Maybe Vast Emptiness.

I'd been playing Bach for years, loved Bach, and could easily have played some that night. Having heard Ramsey Lewis, though, it seemed probable to me that any God in whose image I was made would enjoy him at least as much as I did. Black American rhythm and blues was to Bach, it seemed to me at age twelve, what Mary Magdalene was to Mary—and Jesus loved them both. Ramsey Lewis bent notes, to put it another way, the way Yogi Berra bends words. "Hang On Sloopy" was, at the time, the most exciting piece of music I had in me, and it felt great, making it fly out into the dark sanctuary's Emptiness. The kids for whom I played it loved it, too—till the SDA God's cocksure sergeant at arms came roaring in and filled us all with guilt.

I have never felt the truth of what that man did. I have never understood why the piano's location in "God's House" forbade my choice of song, and have never been able to believe in that enraged man's God. I don't believe I ever will, though the man seems to have cloned himself, bought several broadcasting networks and a political party, and set out to turn all of America, Washington, D.C., first, into a graven image of himself.

Word # 3.   GLADLY

I was reminded of the "Hang On Sloopy" fiasco a few years ago, when I heard about a little boy who'd named his teddy bear Gladly.

"Why Gladly?" someone asked him.

" 'Cause he's cross-eyed," the boy said.

"What's crossed eyes got to do with the name Gladly?" the questioner naturally wondered.

"We sing it at church," the boy explained. "It's a hymn. Called 'Gladly My Cross I'd Bear.'"

I never learned the name of that little boy, though he is, clearly, linguistically related to Yogi Berra. But when I first heard of him and his cross-eyed bear, then thought of Jesus and His terribly unfunny cross, then tried to decide whether there was anything blasphemous about the boy's boyish understanding of the hymn title, I thought at once of Christ's words, "*Whosoever shall not receive the kingdom of God as a little child shall in no wise enter.*" And it occurred to me that if Christ did not find "Gladly My Cross-eyed Bear" funny, even in spite of the manner of His death, His words about the kingdom of God would be a lie.

I have bet my literary and spiritual life on the belief that Christ is not a liar. I have staked my life on an intuition that Jesus *does* find the likes of Gladly funny, and that once upon a time he found another boy's R & B piano palatable, too.

One more story about one more song.

My oldest brother's favorite Christmas carol was "The

Little Drummer Boy." My oldest brother was my best friend when I was a boy. When this brother died at age seventeen, he wasn't worth much in the way of property, but I missed him, "sorely," as the gospels might put it. So I longed to inherit as many as possible of the few things he did own. One of those things was his love for "The Little Drummer Boy." I began to claim it was my favorite Christmas carol.

For a while I was lying about this. For a time my avowed love for "The Little Drummer Boy" was based solely on my love for my vanished brother, and my true favorite carol was a bent-noted, Ramsey Lewis like version of "Good King Wenceslaus" I'd worked out. But as Christmases came and went I kept making up the notion that I loved "The Little Drummer Boy" best, till by God it began to happen that way.

What began to get to me was the song's basic premise. Here is some uninvited urchin, standing right next to the cradle of a newborn baby, banging away on a *drum*. Have any vindictive relatives ever given a child in your home a drum? *Pah rum pah pum pum* is an extremely kind description of the result. Yet, out of reverence and love, this unidentified "poor boy" marches up to the manger of the (probably sleeping) Christ child and bangs the hell out of his drum. The more literally I imagined the impropriety of this drumming, the more it appealed to me: it spoke to the unseemliness of my brother's early death, and to Christ's impending death too. I liked to picture the infant Jesus's eyes, so innocent and new that they were unable to focus, startling wide O-pen at the sudden banging. I liked to picture God the Father wincing On High, wanting to cover His beloved son's ears, make the donkey kick the Drummer Boy senseless, send in the wise men to stop the banging, only to sigh, swallow His anger, and think, "Nope. These are the mortals. This is Earth. This is my beloved son among the mortals on Earth. Let the drummer boy drum."

True, the carol is just a devout work of fiction. It's far from likely that such a scene occurred in Bethlehem. But the song makes it up so truly that later, hasn't it happened that way? If Christ or Rama or the Prophet of God are, as I choose to believe, still alive today, and still listening to anything as multifarious, awkward, and half-baked as the prayers and thoughts we offer them, the small-minded and paltry and disastrous gifts we bring, the wars we offer in Their Name, the slaughter of children we somehow offer in their very Name, doesn't the brutal ear-pounding go on and on and on?

My feeling about God is that our imperfect attempts to worship Him are inevitably and enormously silly, inappropriate, and unworthy. My sense is that God, in His inconceivable Majesty, is being *infinitely* insulted, *all* the time. Yet as I read the world's great Wisdom traditions—Christian, Hebraic, Islamic, Buddhistic, and Vedantic alike—I am filled with wonder to find that God, Love, Vast Emptiness, call It what you will, *requests* this infinity of insults; that, through both Prophet and Son, He reaches so low as to *beg*, from the would-be faithful, every bent-stringed blues note, baby-waking drum beat, and Gladly My Cross-eyed Bear we're able to muster with a whole heart. So every December, the first time I hear "The Little Drummer Boy"—especially when it's sung by kids—the chills run from my spine to my eyes, sometimes spilling over as the truth of the fiction hits home. That it's "a poor boy, too"—same as Jesus, or me, or you: the truth of our spiritual poverty gets me every time. The line, *I played my best for Him pah rum pah pum pum.* What more can one offer, no matter how silly or bad it sounds? The line, *Then He smiled at me pah rum pah pum pum.* What more can we hope for than to please the Vast Emptiness, child king, or little audience we've set out to honor?

I believe—based on the gospels, and on the words of the excommunicated Meister Eckhart and the non-Christian Simone Weil; I believe, based on the beautiful Beguine saints burned at the stake by Christians; I believe, based on the Bhagavad Gita, Sufi poets, *Ramayana, Mahabharata,* Buddhist sutras, and Koran; I believe, based on the bodies of Iraqi, Israeli, and Palestinian children smashed from this world with equal violence by Jewish, Christian, and Muslim bombs; I believe based on intuition, love, prayer, my lifelong experience of our shared spiritual incompetence, and my long-departed brother's favorite Christmas carol—that all human knowledge and praise of God, in relation to He Whom it purports to honor, will forever be so battered and bent-stringed and full of half-truths, untruths, drum whacks, and Yogi Berra-isms that we have no choice but to come unto the Absolute "as little children." This, I'd wager, is exactly why Christ recommends the strategy. It might be nice to come unto Him as Forget-love-and-convert-thy-neighbor "Christian soldiers," or as Armchair Patriots forcing America's disenfranchised to do their Awe-and-Shocking for them, or as perfect-pitched, Pavarotti-voiced angels whose very praise would scare the baby even worse than the drum. But that isn't the drill as the gospels define it.

The God of the gospels and the world's great Wisdom traditions asks His dopey children for every tangled prayer, scrap of inappropriate praise, bent-noted blues ditty, and silence-rending drum whomp they can offer with an honestly whole, honestly confused, honestly divided, or honestly broken heart. And I say thank Allah, thank God, thank Paramatma, Wahtonka, Vast Emptiness, and the Unseen Unborn Guileless Perfection that we're asked.

I believe Jesus was no liar. Which is not to say that the man who threw me out of the old SDA church was. R & B piano, cross-eyed bears named Gladly, and the drumming of poor boys may not belong in such buildings. All I'm saying is that, if they don't, such buildings hold no entry into the kingdom of God.

Unsaying the Word "God"

Who is Jesus? He has no name.

MEISTER ECKHART

It is necessary to define words. It is also at times necessary to undefine them.

One of my aims as a writer of faith is apophatic. From the Greek word *apophasis*.

An *apophasis* is an unsaying.

Out of all the words I have heard in my time, "God" is in my view the one most grievously abused by humans; the one most deserving of a careful *unsaying*.

✦ ✦ ✦

Our love for a person leads us to love the sound of that person's name. I, for example, love a certain woman so much I always thrill slightly at the mere sound of her name. If I heard other people using this name as a pretentious or cruel or polluted exhalation resulting in violence or injustice, if I heard them judging, condemning, even killing each other in the name of my beloved, I would try like hell to defuse this insanity, telling the abusers that this is not what she wants of them and not what her name means.

How, if I love Him, can I do any less for the One nick-named "God"?

. . .

I live on the edge of millions of acres of wilderness. I define wilderness as the parts of our world created by God and not yet flagrantly altered by industrial man. I walk almost daily through places God alone created. While doing so, I see many things that make me feel grateful toward God, but have never once seen a G, O, and D inscribed in His earth or hovering in His water or fluttering in His air. Until I do, I'll continue to believe that this word, "God," is a human creation, and that, because it is human, the word is subject to fallibility. *Allah, Parabrahma, Ehyeh Asher Ehyeh, Ahuramazda, Yezdan, Wahtonka, Gott, Deus, Theos, God*— are but a few of the fallible names for the Be-all and End-all Who infallibly gives us a universe and world and bodies and lives.

The apophatic truth remains: God infinitely transcends all His Names.

. . .

As they emerge from the mouths of men and women, God's names tend to acquire a ponderousness that cannot justly be attributed to the Being to which the names refer. This ponderousness is a result of *human* usage, human thought, ego, self-righteousness, error, feuding, violence. Blaming God for deeds done in His Names strikes me, therefore, as ponderously mistaken. It is humanity's mental preconceptions, delusions, pretensions, so-called righteousness, and cruelties that sully the divine names.

This is why *apophasis* has for thousands of years been an aim of contemplation. Stripped of its ponderousness by an imaginative *unsaying*, the naked sound we make with our mouths—"God"—becomes as innocent as Moses, Jesus, Buddha, or Muhammad as they lay newborn in their mothers' arms, and we are as ready as new mothers to love what we have named.

◆ ◆ ◆

God is Unlimited. Thought and language are limited.

God is the fathomless but beautiful Mystery Who creates the universe and you and me, and sustains it and us every instant, and always shall. The instant we define this fathomless Mystery It is no longer fathomless. To define is to limit. The greater a person's confidence in their definition of God, the more sure I feel that their worship of "Him" has become the worship of their own definition. I don't point this out to insult the fundamentalists' or anyone else's God. I point it out to honor the fathomless Mystery.

◆ ◆ ◆

Why must Creation enter into the human relationship with God?

Meister Eckhart: *If the soul had known God as perfectly as do the angels, it would never have entered the body. And if the soul could have known God without the world, the world would never have been created. The world was made for the soul's sake, so that the soul's eye might be practiced and strengthened to bear the divine light.... The soul's eye could not bear [the divine light] unless it were steadied by matter, supported by likenesses, and so led up to the divine and accustomed to it.*

◆ ◆ ◆

Why must Creation enter into the human relationship with God?

Because theologies are man-made, whereas humans and Creation are not. Revelation is a gift, and the body and Creation are gifts, and each helps us unwrap and cherish the other. Without the Creation-gift to inspire and true us, human belief becomes mere human projection.

The Armageddonist's rejection of the world-as-gift is such a projection: an obsession with the "End Days" is surrender not to God but to men with exaggerated reverence for their own fragmented understanding of holy writ.

We need God in order to love and care for this world, and we need this world to true our love for God. William Blake understood this. Seated, in his old age, beside a little girl at a dinner party, Blake leaned down to her, smiled, and said, "*May God make this world as beautiful to you as it has been to me.*"

We don't know this today because William Blake related it. We know it because Blake's spontaneous words made the world suddenly beautiful to the little girl, and she remembered and recounted his words for the rest of her life.

To every Armageddonist, every earth lover must keep saying with all the sincerity and affection we can muster: "May God make this world as beautiful to you as it has been to me."

...

We need God in order to love and steward creation.
We need Creation to true our love for God.
We also need Creation to better love one another.
The *Song of Solomon* poet understood this:

This form of yours is like a palm tree. . . . I will climb the palm tree, I will take hold of the boughs. May your breasts be as clusters of the vine, your breath as the scent of apples, and your mouth as the choicest wine going down sweetly, my beloved, trickling over the lips of sleepers.

For nonmystical theologians, *The Song of Songs* has proven impossible to interpret, largely because the poems' purposes seem atheological. Mainstream dogmatic theology for the most part denies or distrusts the body and creation, stressing an infinite gulf between God and humans, and citing "the Fall" and "original sin" as the reason for our Maker's harsh judgments against and ceaseless punishment of humanity.

This is why the religious masses are lost without the mystics. Mystics stress not the gulf but the astonishing intimacy between humans and God. "The Word made flesh." Naming each of us "brides" or "lovers," naming God "the Beloved" and Christ "the Groom," mystics perceive love in all its forms as an eternal interplay between lover and Beloved and openly yearn, like the *Song of Songs* poet, not just for heaven but for union with Love Itself.

Mystical yearning in *The Song* is played out in vividly physical bodies. Yet for all their beauty, these bodies are not just mortal objects: they are the essence of the holy homeland and gifts and mysteries of God. In the imagery of *The Song of Songs*, God's art *is* Creation, and the very essence of this art is the body of the human beloved. The beloved's form and incomparably desirable parts, in turn, are described in shockingly specific botanical, biological, and geographical imagery. The love the poet infuses in this imagery then radiates in at least two directions: when the eyes of the beloved are compared to "pools in Heshbon, by the gate of Bathrabbim," legs are likened to "cedars of Lebanon," the head is "Mount Carmel," the breasts "fawns" or "fruits," the lips "honeycomb," the well beneath the tongue "milk and honey," and the breath "apples," we feel both the intricate bliss of lovers lost in one another and the love of an entire people, after long, harsh exile, come home to their promised and holy land.

The result is a spirituality of *Yes!* and *More Yes!* Insofar as the body houses the soul it is holy, and insofar as the body is Creator-given, it is doubly holy, for the body is literally *of* the land; is the physical, spirit-housing essence of the land. This doubled intensity of feeling creates in *The Song* what we might call *an eroticism of loving sacrifice*: in taking the beloved in love, one consumes her; in offering oneself to the beloved, one is consumed; yet what one is offering, receiving, and celebrating is not just one person in a sexual act, it is the herds of the holy hills, the figs, fruits and spices, the orchards, honeycomb, milk, secret gardens, and wells of living waters emphatically seen, in these anything-but-puritanical verses, as components of the physical body. The beloved's body is not just *like* a divine gift: God's giving can be literally touched, felt, and tasted in her body. Through each other, lovers drink, eat, and know the divine gift that is the land.

And where is the line, here, between lovemaking and worship? When the Everything-that-has-made-my-beloved is precisely what and who one yearns for and makes love to, when this same Everything is what one offers her in return, when lovers are effaced in this complete giving and receiving, Who is making love to Whom? To seek and cherish our beloved, as *The Song of Songs* has it, is to seek and cherish, via our bodies, the divine art of the Artist Who gives us bodies. The most complete giver, amid this cherishing, becomes the most complete receiver. *The Song's* "double beloved"—homeland as body and body as homeland—lets us see and feel this. She/He is the spiritual lodestone, and the undying beauty of these poems.

+ + +

Many fundamentalists have no patience for even a word of mystical belief—then wonder why others have no patience for listening to what the fundamentalist believes. I can explain my own such impatience with a parable:

If you were basking in bright sunlight, and hugely thankful for it, and a man a quarter-mile away suddenly shouted, "Hey you! I can see the sun from over here! Stop what you're doing and come over where I am! Hurry! You've GOT to come here! I see the SUN! Come out of your darkness, sinner! Get over to where I am!" is there any reason to obey him? On the contrary, if you obey, you indulge the shouter's peace-shattering belief that the sun is so limited that it can only be seen from where *he* is standing, and you reinforce his false assumption that everyone but he is a fool living in darkness.

Is it the work of sun worshippers to honor those who think only they can see the sun? Or to worship the sun?

+ + +

Terry Tempest Williams:

> *If you know wilderness in the way that you know love, you would be unwilling to let it go. We are talking about the body of the beloved, not real estate.*

John of the Cross:

> *My Beloved is the mountains,*
> *And lonely wooded valleys,*
> *Strange islands,*

And resounding rivers,
The whistling of love-stirring breezes . . .

In the inner wine cellar
I drank of my Beloved, and, when I went abroad,
Through all this valley
I no longer knew anything,
And lost the herd which I was following.

There He gave me His breast;
There He taught me a sweet and living knowledge;
And I gave myself to Him,
Keeping nothing back;
There I promised to be His bride.

Now I occupy my soul
And all my energy in His service;
I no longer tend the herd,
Nor have I any other work
Now that my every act is love.

• • •

The physical world is God's.

The world of imagination is also God's.

To labor in either world with clarity, diligence, humility, humor, and love is a service to God and humanity whether one mentions God while so serving or not.

• • •

How to *unsay* the ponderousness we humans attribute to this word, "God"? How to strip the man-added dreck from the word, that the Being may be loved for Who the Being is?

In the *Upanishads*, God is called "the Unborn, Unseen,

Guileless Perfection." I would love, in my faith life, to become apophatic enough to strip "God" down to this!

If this aim sounds odd to fundamentalist ears, imagine me saying instead that I'd like to journey backward through time with the word "God" until It lies naked in a manger in Bethlehem. It would be as impossible to kill in the name of a word this naked as it would be impossible for the infant in the manger to kill. And it would be as hard not to love a word this naked as it would be hard not to love the infant.

· · ·

The word "God," looked at not as a Being but as an English word, is very simple. Three letters. "Dog" backward.

And the word *is* English, mind you. Three letters of a language invented just a thousand years ago, by Norman conquerors trying to work out a way to command their Anglo-Saxon chattel. To kill or condemn others in the name of a three-letter mongrel Norman/Anglo-Saxon word is tragically absurd. A mortal being who presumes, via the study of holy writ, to know the Mind and Will of Absolute Being is, I think you could literally say, Absolutely mistaken.

There is a way of holding a dogma that sees it as the termination of thought, but religious dogmas (*"There is no God but Allah"*; *"Jesus is the Son of God," " Buddha is the Enlightened One"*) are meant to be windows, not walls, for Infinite Truth infinitely transcends even our best statements about it.

Unforgettable words by Montana's late great fly-fishing philosopher, Henry Bugbee: "The tenets of scripture are meant to be occasions for wonder, not the termination of it."

· · ·

We were given minds that swing from doubt to faith back to doubt back to faith, for a reason. We were given an imagination and a conscience and an intuition for a reason. When a televangelist claims to know the precise meaning of a biblical passage, and his meaning feels to my intuition like a termination of, rather than occasion for, love and wonder, the God in whom I believe encourages me to obey intuition, not the televangelist's or my own frail understanding of the Bible. Otherwise I could end up worshipping—or worse, obeying—nothing more than my misunderstanding of another man's misunderstanding.

There is no book so holy that it cannot be misunderstood and abused. As humans (including me!) demonstrate everywhere, daily, not even God is holy beyond misunderstanding.

· · ·

St. Francis said to God: "No one is worthy to pronounce Thy Name." Jeremiah said of God, "I will not make mention of him, nor speak any more in his name. But his word is in mine heart as a burning fire shut up in my bones."

God is beyond every imagining and mode of expression. Everything we say of Him falls short of Him. Given this common failing, can't we listen to, tolerate, and perhaps even good-naturedly *grin* at the multifarious, contradictory, oft stupid but oft beautiful ways He burns as a fire shut up in our bones?

To wit:

On His infallibility:

Ursula K. Le Guin: *We need the idea of a God who makes mistakes.*

Archie Bunker: *God don't make mistakes. Dat's how He got to be God.*

On His touch:

Tukaram: *God hits you!*
Rumi: *Every instant man receives a slap from the Unseen.*
John Coltrane: *God breathes through us so completely, so gently, we hardly feel it.*

On God and finance:

Billy Graham (speaking of Jesus): *We have a great Commodity here!*
St. Francis (chanting with glee): *For Sister Poverty we give thanks.*
John D. Rockefeller: *God gave me my money.*
Tukaram (singing with glee): *I am bankrupt and God is ruined!*
Gloria Copeland, wife of televangelist Kenneth Copeland: *You give a dollar* [to her and Kenneth's 1,500-acre ranch, private airport, private TV studio, etc.] . . . *for the gospel's sake and the full hundredfold return would be a hundred dollars. . . . A hundredfold return on a thousand dollars would be $100,000.*
Meister Eckhart: *There are those among you who want to see God with the same eyes with which you look at a cow and to love God as you love a cow—for the milk and the cheese.*

On God and gender:

Nancy Litton: *Literally "Shaddai" means "God of the two breasts." God is Almighty because God nurtures, holds all things together, sustains, as a mother would a child in breastfeeding.*

Karen Armstrong: *The masculine tenor of God-talk is particularly problematic in English. In Hebrew, Arabic and French . . . grammatical gender gives theological discourse a sort of sexual counterpoint and dialectic, which provides a balance that is often lacking in English. Thus in Arabic al-Lah—the supreme name for God—is grammatically masculine, but the word for the divine and inscrutable essence of God—al-Dhat—is feminine. All talk about God staggers under impossible difficulties.*

Sherman Alexie (in *Reservation Blues*):

Journalist: "Is God a man or a woman?"

Thomas Builds-the-Fire: "God could be an armadillo. I have no idea."

On the Name itself:

Martin Buber: *We cannot clean up the term "God" and we cannot make it whole; but, stained and mauled as it is, we can raise it from the ground and set it above an hour of great sorrow.*

The Cloud of Unknowing's anonymous author: *No man can think of God himself. It is therefore my wish to leave everything that I can think and choose for my love the thing that I cannot think.*

Herman Melville: *As soon as you say Me, a God, a Nature, so soon you jump off your stool and hang from a beam. . . . Take God out of the dictionary and you would have Him in the street.*

Montaigne: *Man is certainly stark mad. He cannot make a flea, and yet he goes about making gods by the dozen.*

Tukaram:

> *Though You contain the fourteen universes*
> *We fit You in a frame to worship You.*
> *Though You have no definition or form*
> *We display You to show our gratitude to You.*
> *Though You are way beyond words*
> *We sing songs addressed to You.*
> *Though You are apart from all action*
> *We put garlands round Your neck.*
> *Says Tuka: O God, become limited*
> *To pay us a little attention!*

On understanding God:

Walt Whitman: *I understand God not in the least.*
Mother Teresa: *I do not understand the ways of God.*

> Joshu: *Should I turn to the way or not?*
> Nansen: *If you turn to it, then you're going against it.*
> Joshu: *If I don't turn to the way, how can I know that it is the way?*
> Nansen: *The way does not belong to knowing or not-knowing.*

> Meister Eckhart: *The more one seeks God, the less one finds him. You should seek him in a way that you find him nowhere. . . . Man should not be satisfied with a thought-of God, for when the thought fades away, so does the God. . . . When people think they are acquiring more of God in inwardness, in devotion, in sweetness, and in various approaches than they do by the fireside or in the stable, it is just as if they are taking God and muffling his head up in a cloak and shoving him under a bench. Whoever is seeking God by ways is finding ways and losing God, who in ways is hidden.*

On the existence of God:

Simone Weil: *It's a case of contradictions, both of them true. There is a God. There is no God. Where is the problem? I am quite sure there is a God in the sense that I am sure my love is no illusion. I am quite sure there is no God in the sense that I am sure there is nothing which resembles whatever I conceive when I say that word.*

Tukaram:
> *The main message is absolutely clear:*
> *This whole world is God.*
> *First, scatter your own ego to the winds.*
> *Then you will pass the crucial test.*
> *The decisive thing to know about Absolute Being?*
> *Says Tuka: Once the mind is blown up,*
> *There is neither a cause nor an effect.*

Eckhart: *The Holy Scriptures shout that man should be freed from self, for being freed from self you are self-controlled, and as you are self-controlled you are self-possessed, and as you are self-possessed you possess God and all creation. I tell you the truth: as sure as God is God and I am man, if you could be freed of self—as free as you are of the highest angels—then you would have the nature of the highest angels as completely as you now have your own.*

On the unspeakable nature of God:

Ruzbihan Baqli: *His eternity has no measurable beginning. . . . Substances and accidents vanish in the fields of his oneness, and spirits and intellects are annihilated in the courtyards of his splendor. . . . His attributes are sanctified beyond the comprehension of intellects and imaginations. He was by virtue of his divinity before every existing being,* and he will be by virtue of his power after all limits are passed. *Lofty aspirations do not plumb the fullness of his depth, and searching intelligence does not scale the heaven of his attributes. There is no penetration of the secrets of his majesty, nor is there any comprehension of the lights of his beauty. The sublimities of his greatness obliterate vision, and the assaults of his magnificence erases thought. The power of his everlastingness confounds temporal understanding, and the wrath of his unity overpowers the contraints of space.*

On loving God:

Simone Weil: *In the period of preparation for loving God, the soul loves in emptiness. It does not know whether anything real answers its love. It may believe that it knows, but to believe is not to know. Such a belief does not help. The soul knows for certain only that it is hungry. The important thing is that it announces its hunger by crying. A child does not stop crying if we suggest to it that perhaps there is no such thing as bread. It goes on crying just the same. The danger is not lest the soul should doubt whether there is bread, but lest, by a lie, it should persuade itself that it is not hungry. It can only persuade itself of this by lying, for the reality of its hunger is not a belief, it is a certainty.*

Mahatma Gandhi: *Give us your Christ and keep your Christianity.*

John of the Cross: *In the end we are judged by love.*

3

• • • • • • • •

What Fundamentalists Need
for Their Salvation

Go forth and preach. And if you have to, use words.

ST. FRANCIS OF ASSISI

1. Censored

A few years ago I was asked to speak to sixty or seventy high
school students in a town neither geographically nor de-
mographically far from Sweet Home, Oregon, from whence
the Oregon Citizens Alliance—a fundamentalist religious
group with a selective-Leviticus-quoting antihomosexual
agenda—had sprung into national headlines. The high
school was in a logging town and I'm a defender of our last
few remaining ancient forests. I was years behind on a novel
deadline, and busy with my own three kids. I accepted the
invitation anyhow, when I learned that students were being
forced to read a version of my first novel, *The River Why*,
from which hundreds of words had been purged by a team
of parents armed with indelible black felt-tip pens.

The general topic of this novel is, for lack of a better
word, *redemption*—the redemption, in this case, of a young
fly fisherman. The genre is ancient: the story of a spiritual

quest. The novel had already been assigned, a teacher explained to me when I arrived at the school, and her class was halfway through it, when the mother of a student happened to pick the book up and discover my protagonist's use of language. By no stretch of the imagination or Bible could his language be considered obscene. Using the Hollywood rating system, I believe my novel would receive a "PG-13" — and I'm embarrassed to add that a "G" would be as likely as an "R." The passages this mother nevertheless proceeded to underline, xerox, and distribute at a P.T.A. meeting nearly caused the book to be banned outright. At the same meeting, however, a couple of brave English teachers stood up and tenaciously defended the morality of the novel's overall aims, enabling a compromise (which of course satisfied neither side) to be reached. The book was called back from the students, duly purged by the parents, and reassigned. Then, as some sort of finale (and, I think, an act of teacherly revenge upon the vigilantes), I was invited to visit.

Upon arriving at the school, the first thing I did was paw through an excised copy to see just how black my prose had been deemed to be—and more than a few pages, it turned out, looked rather as if Cajuns had cooked them. But what interested me far more than the quantity of black marks was the unexpected difficulty of the whole censorship endeavor. Hard as these parents had tried to Clorox my prose, a myopic focus on "nasty words" at the expense of attention to narrative flow had resulted in a remarkably self-defeating arbitrariness. They'd taken care, for instance, to spare their big strapping logging-town teenagers my protagonist's dislike of the Army Corps of Engineers by converting the phrase "God damn dams" to "God [beep] dams." Yet when the same protagonist, one Gus Orviston, told a story about an inch-and-a-half-long scorpion his kid brother lost inside his fly-fishing-crazed family's house, not a word was blackened out of Gus's surmise that the lonely creature had ultimately "found and fallen in love with one of my father's mayfly imitations and died of lover's nuts trying to figure out how to screw the thing."

Along similar lines, Gus was allowed, in a scene when his lady-love rejected him, to describe himself as a "blubbering Sasquatch . . . my beard full of lint, my teeth yellow, my fly open and undershorts showing there the same color as my teeth, and thick green boogers clogging both my nostrils." Yet when he attempted moments later to describe the bottom of a river as "the place where the slime and mudsuckers and fish-shit live," student innocence had to be protected by the prophylactic "fish-[beep]."

The pattern grew obvious: while my protagonist had been allowed to piss, puke, and fornicate, to insult door-to-door evangelists, and even to misread and reject the Bible with impunity, every time he tried to use a so-called dirty word—even the innocuous likes of "hell," "damn," or "ass"—down came the indelible markers. Some kind of "suitable-for-mixed-company" politeness was all that my censors were out to impose. It always seems to dumbfound and offend the promulgators of such cleanlinesses when the makers and defenders of literature declare even purges like theirs to be not just ineffective, but dangerous.

The students' reactions to being assigned censored literature turned out to be mild compared to their teachers'. Most considered it embarrassing to be "treated like kids" in this way, but no more embarrassing than many other facets of high school, small town, and family life. When I read to them the novel's single most censored scene—an exposé of the greed and stupidity of two drunken and foul-mouthed fishermen—with the foul words restored, the students, on a show of hands, unanimously preferred greedy drunks to sound like greedy drunks, not Sunday School teachers. They also agreed that the purge had been ineffective, since their imaginations had readily supplied every blacked-out word. But most of them were no more able than their parent-censors to perceive or articulate any real danger in the laundering of their curriculum or literature.

A parable on the danger:

When I was a kid and picked raspberries for money, some of the teenaged boys in the fields used to defy the heat, boredom, and row bosses (most of whom were staid Judeo-Suburban housewives) by regaling us with a series of ad-libbed yarns they called "The Adventures of One-Eyed Dirk." To a casual listener, One-Eyed Dirk's were some of the dullest adventures ever endured. We pickers listened with bated breath, though, knowing it was our teen raconteurs, not Dirk, who were having the real adventure. The trick to a One-Eyed Dirk story was to juxtapose strategic verbs and modifiers with names of common nouns (say, car parts, office supplies, or garden vegetables) in a way that, through the magic of metaphor, let you spout pure analogical pornography within the hearing of all, yet proclaim your innocence if confronted by an offended adult. An example might go: "Stunned by the size of the musk melons she'd offered him, One-Eyed Dirk groped through his own meager harvest, found the bent green zucchini, sighed at the wormhole in the end, but, with a shy smile, drew it out and thrust it slowly toward her . . ."

Silly as this kind of thing may be, it underscores the fact that there is virtually nothing a would-be censor can do to guarantee the purity of language, because it is not just words that render language impure. Even "dirty" words tend to be morally neutral until placed in a context—and it is the individual human imagination, more than individual words, that gives a context its moral or immoral twist. One-Eyed Dirk's G-rated zucchinis and wing nuts and valve jobs drive home the point that a bored kid out to tell an off-color yarn can do it with geometry symbols, nautical flags, or two rocks and a stick if he wants. The human imagination was *designed* (by its Designer, if you will) to make rapid-fire, free-form, often preposterous connections between shapes, words, colors, ideas, desires, sounds. This is its seeming "moral weakness," but also its wondrous strength. The very nature of imagination is the reason why organized censorship never quite works—and also the reason why every ferociously determined censorship effort sooner or later escalates into fascistic political agendas, burnings at the stake, dunking chairs, gulags, pogroms, and other literal forms of purge. Obviously, the only fail-safe way to eliminate impurities from human tongues, imaginations, and cultures is to eliminate human life itself.

2. The Morality of Literature

Ever since the advent of the printing press, there have been readers who slip from enthusiasm for a favorite text into the belief that the words in that text embody truth: do not just symbolize it, but *literally embody it*. Not till the past century, though, has an American alliance of self-styled "conservative Christians" declared that this slip is in fact the true Christian religion, that a single bookful of words is Absolute Truth, and that this Truth should become the sole basis of the nation's political, legal, and cultural life. The growing clout of this faction does not change the theological aberrance of its stance: fundamentalism's deification of the written words of the Bible—in light of every scripture-based Wisdom tradition in the world *including Christianity's two-thousand-year-old own*—is not just naïveté: it is idolatry.

Words in books can remind us of truth, and help awaken us to it. But in themselves, words are just paint and writers are just painters, Old Testament and gospel writers, bhakti and Sufi saints, Tibetan lamas and Catholic popes included. There are, of course, crucial differences between scripture and belles lettres, and between inspired and merely inventive prose. But the authors of both write with human hands and in human tongues.

Let us not overestimate the power of any form of literature.

Let us not underestimate it either. As readers we are asked on page one to lay our hand upon the back of an author's as he or she paints a world. If the author's strokes somehow repel or betray our trust, if our concentration is lax, or if we're biased or closed in some way, then no hand-in-hand magic can occur. But when a great word-painter is read with reciprocally great concentration and trust, a wondrous thing happens. First, the painter's hand disappears. Then so does our own. Till there is only the living world of the painting.

This disappearance—this effacement of self in the life of a story—is, I believe, the greatest truth we experience through any literature, be it discursive or dramatic, sacred or secular. It is, at any rate, the greatest *describable* truth we experience, since for the duration of our effacement we possess no "I" with which to describe anything outside the imagined world in which we've become lost. Like all great truths, this disappearance of self in an interior world requires, simultaneously, a sacrifice (of the reader's ego) and a resurrection (of the world and characters in the text). And like all great truths, it is not realized by picking and choosing certain literal meanings from the text's sentences and words: what is required is a willing immersion of imagination, intuition, and mind in the dynamic pulse and flow of living language.

In light of this truth, the most valid form of censorship is that practiced by writers upon themselves. Scrupulously revising or destroying all writing that fails to let readers vanish into the life of their language is every author's duty. What we are morally obligated to censor from our work, in other words, is our own incompetence. Nothing more, nothing less. Simple as it sounds, it keeps us more than busy. "Fundamental accuracy of statement," wrote Ezra Pound in support of this brand of censorship, "is the one sole morality of literature." If, in other words, a story requires that its author create a mountain, and further requires that this mountain be imposing, the immoral mountain is not the one with the pair of unmarried hikers copulating on a remote slope: it is the mountain that fails to be imposing. The "sole morality of literature" demands that an author contemplate his peak till frozen clouds begin to swirl round the summit, frigid stone masses haunt and daunt us, and the bones of fallen climbers and mountain goats appear not at some safe distance but in the crevasses at our very feet.

With all due apologies to literary inquisitors everywhere, the same "one sole morality" applies in regard to the imposing penis. This is not to say that all penises are, according to Pound's dictum, moral. Indeed, a gratuitously shocking penis, an extraneous-to-our-story penis, a hey-look-at-me-for-the-sake-of-nothing-but-me penis, however imposing, is literarily immoral (that is, incompetent), since by jarring the reader from the narrative flow into a mood of "What's this stupid penis doing here?" the author has undermined the greatest truth of his tale—that is, our ability to immerse ourselves in it. Once the dramatic exigencies of a story have demanded of its author an imposing penis, however, it is the apoplectic-veined archetype that has us defensively crossing imaginary legs before we know it (or opening them, as the narrative case may be) that is the literarily moral penis. And it is the church, quasi-religious political cult, or government agency that seeks to drape a cloth over it that is, literarily, immoral.

But how could the deletion of male members, filthy language, perversion, sadomasochism, sexual violence, and so on ever be criticized? Why in God's name shouldn't we censor literature, art, and human behavior itself in order to safeguard the innocence of our children and our culture? These are the "purity questions," the "morality questions"—the Jesse Helms, Jerry Falwell, Pat Robertson questions, yes, and also the Stalin, Hitler, Mao, McCarthy, Khomeini, Taliban questions. Libertarians and knee-jerk liberals need to remind themselves, however, that a lot of people besides fanatics and ideologues ask the same questions—all responsible parents of young children, for instance.

Here are two sincere answers to the purity questions, one civic, one Christian.

The civic:

To seek laws that protect each citizen's freedom of expression is not to seek a citizenry that freely expresses anything and everything. Art and literature at their worst can be depraved. But the citizens of this country *already* possess a Constitutional right to say so: we are perfectly free, regardless of our religion, to detest the work of any writer or artist we honestly detest, and to criticize that writer or artist in the most scathing language we're able to devise. I, for example, found the few chapters of Bret Easton Ellis's *American*

Psycho I got through to be as sensationalistic and literarily incompetent as any novel I've ever tried to read. To "shock and awe" readers by torturing characters redundantly and without mercy is not a literary strategy to which "the one sole morality of literature" allows most writers to subscribe. But to say this much satisfies me. And it's all the fun the Constitution allows. To carry my disgust further—to try to summon the outrage, compose the propaganda, induce the paranoia, and generate the political clout that would let me and my ideological clones ban, purge, or punish one overpaid hack—is not the way people in this tenuously free country long ago agreed to do things.

The church, historically, has ruled many a state, and has generally not ruled well. This is precisely why America now does things differently. As James Madison observed in 1785, "ecclesiastical establishments" have upheld many political tyrants, and they have created many spiritual tyrannies, but "in no instance have they been seen [to be] the guardians of the liberties of the people. . . . A just Government instituted to secure & perpetuate [liberty] needs them not." America's founding fathers decided, in short, that self-restraint, while far from perfect, is infinitely preferable to being restrained by priests and kings.

The greatest literature practices such restraint. The old Irish bards, for instance, when asked to recite certain vile stories, would often say to their audience: *'Tis an evil tale for telling. I canna' make it.* And hearing this, the crowd would request a different tale. Hyperconfessional and sensation-addicted Americans could use a dose of this bardic wisdom. But sickening stories remain an unavoidable by-product of sick cultures, and a crucial diagnostic tool for anyone seeking a cure. Writers need the freedom to invoke mayhem, sexuality, moral ambiguities, and twisted visions for as many reasons as chefs need the freedom to invoke curry, garlic, Chinese mustard, and other substances we can't tolerate in large doses, in order to produce a fine cuisine. There is no mention of jalapeño peppers in the Bible, and neither the average child or average televangelist can handle them: this is no reason to legislate them clean out of our huevos rancheros.

The Christian answer to the purity question:

In the slender classic, *An Experiment in Criticism*, that indefatigably Christian lover of non-Christian literature, C. S. Lewis, wrote that access to uncensored literature is crucial because we are not meant to be imprisoned in a single, isolated self. "We demand windows," he wrote. "[And] literature . . . is a series of windows, even of doors. . . . Good reading . . . can be described either as an enlargement or as a temporary annihilation of the self. But that is an old paradox; 'he that loseth his life shall save it.' We therefore delight to enter into other men's beliefs . . . even though we think them untrue. And into their passions, though we think them depraved. . . . Literary experience heals the wound, without undermining the privilege, of individuality. . . . In reading great literature I become a thousand men and yet remain myself. . . . Here—as in worship, in love, in moral action, and in knowing—I transcend myself, and am never more myself than when I do."

3. Why No Argument against Fundamentalist Censorship Works

The majority of challenges to the printed word in American schools, libraries, and bookstores are made by people who call themselves "fundamentalist" or "evangelical" Christians. I've just provided two arguments against such challenges. I don't believe, however, that my arguments, or any argument resembling them in category, will persuade a single committed fundamentalist that censorship is a potentially deadly cultural strategy. The only way to persuade a fundamentalist of such a thing would be with a fundamentalist argument. And there are none. Fundamentalism and censorship have always gone hand in hand.

My focus here is literary, not theological. But for literary reasons I am compelled to point out that a theologically simplistic, politically motivated, mass-produced cult is out to simplify and "improve" our literature, art, science, sexual choices, Constitution, culture, and souls, and that I see no more effective choice, in defending ourselves against these "improvements," than to confront the theological basis of the cult itself. By confining ourselves to trying to defend those whom organized fundamentalism attacks—gays and evolutionists, for example—we feed ourselves right into the teeth of the "Christian Right's" propaganda machinery. I know poets and authors capable of making a crowd weep at the sincerity and beauty of their art. Every time I see one of them reduced to publically explaining, via blurts of verbiage nonsensically edited by some TV news show, that they're trying to defend freedom of expression, not the freedom of perverts and pedophiles, I feel a huge strategic error being committed. Literary people, being comparatively complex, seem mystified by the adamant oversimplifications that fuel fundamentalist attacks on scientific truth and artistic and civil freedoms. Having lived among fundamentalists, I don't understand this mystification. The belligerent mind-set and self-insulating dogmas that enable politicized fundamentalism to proliferate are neither complicated nor invulnerable to criticism. To treat the earth as disposable and the Bible as "God," turn that "God" into a political action committee, equate arrogance and effrontery with "evangelism," right-wing politics with "worship," aggression with "compassion," disingenuous televised prattle with "prayer," and call the result "Christianity," is, as I read the words and acts of Jesus, not an enviable position, but a fatal one.

Rather than try to defend welfare mothers, valid science, loving gay couples, Muslim culture, fragile ecosystems, or any other scapegoat or victim of fundamentalist rhetoric, I'd like to take a closer look at the scapegoat manufacturers themselves.

4. American Fundamentalism

Most of the famed leaders of the new "Bible-based" American political alliances share a conviction that their causes and agendas are approved of, and directly inspired, by no less a being than God. This enviable conviction is less enviably arrived at by accepting on faith, hence as "higher-than-fact," that the Christian Bible pared down into American TV English is God's "word" to humankind, that this same Bible is His only word to humankind, and that the politicized apocalyptic fundamentalist's unprecedentedly selective slant on this Bible is the one true slant.

The position is remarkably self-insulating. Possessing little knowledge of or regard for the world's wealth of religious, literary, spiritual, and cultural traditions, fundamentalist leaders allow themselves no concept of love or compassion but their own. They can therefore honestly, even cheerfully, say that it is out of "Christian compassion" and a sort of "tough love" for others that they seek to impose on all others their tendentiously literalized God, Bible, and slant. But how tough can love be before it ceases to be love at all? Well-known variations on the theme include the various

Inquisitions' murderously tough love for "heretics" who for centuries were defined as merely defiant of the Inquisition itself; the European Catholic and American Puritan tough love for "witches" who for centuries were defined as virtually any sexually active or humanitarian or unusually skilled single woman whose healing herbs or independence from men defied a male church hierarchy's claim to be the source of all healing; the Conquistadors' genocidally tough love for the Inca, Aztecs, and Maya whose gold they stole for the "glory" of a church meant to honor the perfect poverty of a life begun in a manger and ended on a cross; the missionaries' and U.S. cavalry's genocidally tough love for land-rich indigenous peoples whose crime was merely to exist; and, today, the Bush team's murderously tough love for an oil-rich Muslim world as likely to convert to Texas neocon values as Bush himself is likely to convert to Islam.

Each of these crusader groups has seen itself as fighting to make its own or some other culture "more Christian" even as it tramples the teachings of Christ into a blood-soaked earth. The result, among millions of nonfundamentalists, has been a growing revulsion toward anything that chooses to call itself "Christian." But I see no more crucial tool for defusing fundamentalist aggression than the four books of the gospels, and can think of no more crucial question to keep asking self-righteous crusaders than whether there is anything truly imitative of Jesus—that is, anything compassionate, self-abnegating, empathetic, forgiving, and enemy-loving—in their assaults on religious and cultural diversity, ecosystem health, non-Christian religion, or anything else they have determined to be "evil."

For two thousand years the heart of Christianity has *not* been a self-pronounced "acceptance of Jesus as my personal lord and savior": the religion's heart has been the words, example, and Person of Jesus, coupled with the believer's unceasing attempt to speak, act, and live in accord with this sublime example. (*"This life is not good if it is not an imitation of His life."*—John of the Cross) When the word "Christian" sinks beneath this definition—when a mere self-proclaimed formula is said to suffice for salvation, enabling "saved Christians" to behave in a far less Christ-like manner than millions who consider themselves non-Christian—what has the term "Christian" come to mean?

Jesus's words and sacrifice point humanity both to Himself and beyond Himself, for the Person of Jesus, traditionally, opens directly into the Unbounded. A "personal relationship" with such a being is not something one can "exclusively" own: what the Person of Jesus invites His followers into is a loving relationship with Infinite Mystery. I find it hard to see this Mystery operating in the cocksure judgments, financial scheming, and propagandizing of "evangelists" such as Kenneth Copeland, Pat Robertson, Robert Tilton, Benny Hinn, and Jerry Falwell. Indeed, Christ's Sermon on the Mount is rife with warnings against their kind of proselytizing. (*"Not everyone that saith unto me, Lord, Lord, shall enter into the kingdom of heaven." "Hypocrites . . . love to pray standing in the synagogues and in the corners of the streets, that they may be seen of men." "Whosoever shall not receive the kingdom of God as a little child shall in no wise enter." "Thou hypocrite, first cast out the beam that is of thine own eye; and then shalt thou see clearly to cast the mote out of thy brother's eye."*)

As for the political side of the neocon/fundamentalist fusion, Christ's Beatitudes bless the poor in spirit, they that mourn, the meek, the merciful, the pure in heart, and the peacemakers, among others. What merciful peacemaker can claim to see these blessings manifesting in the conservation debacles, the support of the superrich, and the war making of George W. Bush? I'm not averse to a little Bible-thumping. What appalls me is the deletion of Christ's loving example from the Jesus-character in the Bible that politicized fundamentalists choose to thump. Jesus practiced no politics, spoke of no left or right, and commited no acts of violence, however justified. His embrace of humanity included everyone, though He sternly and repeatedly warned the ungenerous rich, the self-righteously religious, and "hypocrites" of the errors of their ways. The daily stance He repeatedly encouraged was to remain childlike, grateful, loving, and endlessly forgiving. His parables were profoundly mystical, His literalism nonexistent.

Another problem with fundamentalist "tradition": a mere ninety years ago the word "fundamentalist" did not exist: the term was coined by an American Protestant splinter group which, in 1920, proclaimed that adhering to "the literal inerrancy of the Bible" was the true Christian faith. The popularity of this blunder does not change the gospel facts. Deifying the mere letter of biblical law blinds the believer to the spirit we see again and again in Jesus's loving words, deeds, and example.

This, in all sincerity, is why American fundamentalists need connections to, and the compassion of, those who are no such thing. How can those lost in literalism save one another? As Max Weber put it: "We [Christians] are building an iron cage, and we're inside of it, and we're closing the door. And the handle is on the outside."

5. Inside the Cage

Contemporary American fundamentalism is in many ways a manufactured product, and in some ways even an industrial by-product. While its grandiosity of scale is impressive, so is McDonald's, Coca-Cola's, and ExxonMobil's. Its fully auto-mated evangelical machinery runs twenty-four hours a day, like any factory, making "converts" globally. But to what? The conversion industry's notion of the word Christian has substituted a "Rapture Index" and Armageddon fantasy for Christ's interior kingdom of heaven and love of neighbor; it is funded by donors lured by a televangelical "guarantee" of "a hundredfold increase on all financial donations," as if Mark 10:30 were an ad for a financial pyramid scheme and Jesus never said, "Sell all thou hast and distribute unto the poor"; it has replaced once-personal relationships between parishioners and priests or preachers with radio and TV bombast, sham healings, and congregation-fleecing scams performed by televangelical "rock stars"; it has trumped worship characterized by contemplative music, reflective thought, and silent prayer with three-ring media circuses and "Victory Campaigns"; it inserts veritable lobbyists in its pulpits and political brochures in its pews, claims that both speak for Jesus, and raises millions for this "Jesus" though its version of him preaches neocon policies straight out of Washington think tanks and spends most of "his" money on war; it quotes Mark 10:15 and Matthew 5:44 and Matthew 6:6 and Luke 18:9–14 a grand total of never; it revels in its election of a violent, historically ignorant, science-flaunting, carcinogenic-policied president who goads us toward theoc-racy at home even as he decries theocracies overseas; it de-fies cooperation and reason in governance, exults in division, and hastens the degeneration of a democracy built upon cooperation and reason; it claims an exclusive monopoly on truth (*"This ideal of America is the hope of all mankind."* —G. W. Bush) yet trivializes truth globally by evincing ig-norance of Christianity's historical and spiritual essence, disrespect toward the world's ethnic and religious diversity, and a stunning lack of interest in humanity's astonishingly rich cultural present and past.

To refer to peregrinating Celtic monks and fundamentalist lobbyists, Origen and Oral Roberts, the Desert Fathers and Tim LaHaye, Dante and Tammy Faye, St. Francis and the TV "Prosperity Gospel" hucksters, Lady Julian of Norwich and Jimmy Swaggart, John of the Cross and George W. Bush, all as "Christian" stretches the word so thin its meaning vanishes. The term "carbon-based life-form" is as informative. The gulf between historic Christianity and politicized, media-driven fundamentalism is *vast*. Misreading its one book, condescending to all others, using the resultant curtailment of comprehension and tolerance as a unifying principle, industrialized fundamentalism seeks to control minds, not open them; seeks the tithe-paying ideological clone, not C. S. Lewis's "windows into others"; seeks a rigidification and righteousness of self, not literature's enlargement of self, or Christ's recommended effacement of it.

"United" in this way, we shall fall.

But to merely shun those trapped inside this ideology is also futile. Those who are not fundamentalists are too often satisfied with expressing derision, intellectual superiority, or revulsion toward them and calling it good. John of the Cross proposes a more difficult but promising course of action: *"Have a great love for those who contradict and fail to love you, for in this way love is begotten in a heart that has no love. God so acts with us, for He loves us that we might love by means of the very love He bears toward us."*

6. Shame and Reverence

The hero of my censored novel, Gus by name, was a fly fisher and spiritual seeker who voiced serious reservations about the Being some believers so possessively refer to as "God." But a problem that Gus and I ran into in telling his story was that, after a climactic all-night adventure with a river and a huge chinook salmon, he had a sudden, transrational (or, in the old Christian lexicon, "mystical") experience that left him too overwhelmed to speak with accuracy, yet too grateful to remain mute. This paradox is autobiographical. As the recipient of many such detonations, I felt bound by gratitude to let my protagonist speak of such mysteries. But as a lifelong witness of the fundamentalist assault on the Christian lexicon, I felt compelled to speak in non-Christian terms. Though Gus spoke of a presence so God-like that in the end he dubbed it "the Ancient One," his account of his experience did not once invoke the word "God."

Reader reactions to this climax have been neatly divided. Those who have experienced similar detonations have sometimes been so moved by the scene that their eyes filled as they thanked me for writing it—and those who've experienced no such detonation have asked why I ruined a dang good fishin' yarn with woowoo. I admire both reactions. Both are constitutionally correct. Both are perfectly honest. What more should a writer want from his reader? What more, for that matter, can a mortal, be they skeptic or mystic, offer the Absolute?

The French novelist-philosopher René Daumal describes the paradox I faced perfectly. He wrote: "I swear to you that I have to force myself to write or to pronounce this word: God. It is a noise I make with my mouth or a movement of the fingers that hold my pen. To pronounce or to write this word makes me ashamed. What is real here is that shame. Must I never speak of the Unknowable because it would be a lie? Must I speak of the Unknowable because I know that I proceed from it and am bound to bear witness to it? This contradiction is the prime mover of my best thoughts."

Another word for this shame, in my view, is *reverence*. And fundamentalism, speaking of the Unknowable, too often lacks this essential quality. The kind of fundamentalism that now more or less governs our country does not just proudly pronounce the word "God," it defines and Americanizes "God," worships its own definition, and aims to impose that definition on all. What an abyss between this effrontery and the Christ-inspired self-giving of a St. Francis, Mother Teresa, or Martin Luther King! What a contrast, too, between this kind of Christianity and that of the Amish, who practice no evangelism, who tease those who quote the Bible too often (calling them "scripture smart"), and who consider it laughable to pronounce oneself "saved," since God alone is capable of such almighty judgments.

And what a gulf between fundamentalism and American literature. If America's writers have arrived at a theological consensus concerning what humans owe the Divine, it might be this: better to be honest to God, even if that means stating one's complete lack of belief in any such Being, than to allow one's mind and imagination to be processed by an ideology factory—be it fundamentalist, Marxist, or what have you. E. B. White said it well: "In a free country it is the duty of writers to pay no attention to duty. Only under a dictatorship is literature expected to exhibit an harmonious design or an inspirational tone."

The "inspirational art" of the Maoist opera and the "Christian Supply Store" are equally blind, in their dutiful purpose, to the truth that God works in mysterious ways. In literature as in life, for example, there are ways of disbelieving in God that are more loving, and in this sense more imitative of Jesus, than some forms of orthodox belief. There are agnostic and atheist humanitarians who believe as they do, and love their neighbors as they do, because the cruelty of humanity makes it impossible for them to conceive of a God who is anything but remiss or cruel. Rather than consider God cruel, they choose doubt or disbelief, and serve others anyway. This is a backhanded form of reverence; a beautiful kind of "shame."

It seems to upset some fundamentalists that literature's answer to "the God question" is as open-minded as the Constitution's, and that most writers remain as determined as were the founding fathers to separate church from state. There is also no doubt that the openness our literature and Constitution encourage results in a theological cacophony and mood of irritable interdependence that bear little resemblance to the self-righteousness now reigning in the average conservative church. But America remains a country that stakes its life and literature on the belief that this cacophony and interdependence are not only legal, but essential to our health.

Edward Abbey remains welcome to say: "*God is Love? Not bloody likely!*" Goethe remains welcome to reply: "*As a man is, so is his God; therefore God is often an object of mockery.*" And the readers of both—provided they avoid thought-control machines—remain free to draw their own intelligent conclusions.

7. What Fundamentalists Need for Their Salvation

There is one precious Earth, and she is finite. She can absorb just so many wounds or poisons before she ceases to support life. Millions of us have recognized that in wounding the earth for centuries we have been wounding ourselves, and that the only "kingdom of God" to which Christ gives directions lies within these wounded selves. There is likewise, for most humans born on earth, just one mother tongue, and it is less widely recognized that a given tongue at a given time consists of only so many words, and that these words can absorb only so many abuses before they cease to mean.

America's spiritual vocabulary—with its huge defining terms such as "God," "soul," "sacrifice," "mysticism," "faith," "salvation," "grace," "redemption"—has been enduring a series of abuses so constricting that the damage may last for centuries. Too many of us have tried to sidestep this damage by simply rejecting the terminology. The defamation of a religious vocabulary cannot be undone by turning away: the harm is undone when we work to reopen each word's true history, nuance, and depth. Holy words need stewardship as surely as do gardens, orchards, or ecosystems. When lovingly tended, such words surround us with spaciousness and mystery the way a sacred grove surrounds us with cathedral light, peace, and oxygenated air. When we merely abandon our holy words, and fail to replace them, we end up living in a spiritual clear-cut.

If Americans of European descent are to understand and honor the legacy of Celtic, European, Middle Eastern, and other Christian traditions and pass our literature, music, art, monasticism, and mysticism on intact, the right-wing hijacking of Christianity must be defined as the reductionist rip-off that it is. To allow televangelists or pulpit neocons to claim exclusive ownership of Jesus is to hand that incomparable lover of enemies, prostitutes, foreigners, children, and fishermen over to those who evince no such love. And to cede the word "Christian" to earth-trashing literalists who say "the End is nigh" feels rather like ceding my backyard henhouse to weasels. For my hens (and morning omelettes), such a concession would sure enough bring on "the end of the world." But neither my chickens nor I consider the end of our world something to yearn for and work toward.

The God of politicized right-wing fundamentalism, as advertised daily by a relentless array of media, is a Supramundane Caucasian Male as furious with humanity's failure to live by a few randomly selected dictums from Leviticus as He is oblivious to the "Christian Right's" failure to live the compassion of the gospels and earth stewardship of both testaments. As surely as I feel love and need for food and water, I feel love and need for God. But these feelings have nothing to do with Supramundane Males planning torments for those who don't abide by neocon "moral values." If the "Christian Right's God" is indeed God, then all my spiritual heroes from Valmiki and Laotse, Bodhidharma and Socrates, Kabir and Mira Bai, Rumi and Hafiz, Dogen and Dante, Teresa of Avila and Julian of Norwich, Eckhart and the Beguines, Sankaracharya and Aquinas, Black Elk and Chief Joseph, Tolstoy and Dostoevsky, Thoreau and Muir, Shunryu and D. T. Suzuki, Gandhi and the Dalai Lama, to Merton and Snyder, will be consigned to perdition with me—for the One we all worship is an infinitely more loving, infinitely less fathomable Being.

Based on the lives and words of the preceding heroes and on the Person and gospels of Jesus Himself, I believe humanity's situation to be rather different. I hold the evangelical truth of the matter to be that contemporary fundamentalists, including first and foremost those aimed at Empire and Armageddon, need us nonfundamentalists, mystics, ecosystem activists, unprogrammable artists, agnostic humanitarians, incorrigible writers, truth-telling musicians, incorruptible scientists, organic gardeners, slow food farmers, gay restaurateurs, wilderness visionaries, pagan preachers of sustainability, compassion-driven entrepreneurs, heartbroken Muslims, grief-stricken children, loving believers, loving disbelievers, peace-marching millions, and the One who loves us all in such a huge way that it is not going too far to say *they need us for their salvation.*

As Mark Twain pointed out over a century ago, the only truly prominent community that fundamentalists have so far established in any world, real or imaginary, is hell.

4

* * * * * * * *

When Compassion Becomes Dissent

written in October & November 2002

I.

I have been serving my country, this deceptively serene Rocky Mountain autumn, as a visiting instructor of creative writing at the University of Montana. I lead two classes, each three hours long, with twenty students all told. My students are not "aspiring writers" exactly: they're the real thing, and in two months' time their collective intensity, wit, and talent have lifted our joint undertaking into the realm of arduous but steady pleasure. Yet as the semester unfolds and we listen to President Bush and his various goaders and backers wage a rhetorical war on Iraq and prepare an increasingly vague national "we" to lay waste to Saddam Hussein possibly, and to civilians and children inevitably, the teaching of creative writing has come to feel, for the first time in my life, like a dissident line of work.

Creative writing requires a dual love of language and of life, human and otherwise. The storyteller then sculpts these raw loves with acute observation, reflection, creative struggle, allegiance to truth, merciless awareness of the foibles of human beings, and unstinting empathy toward human beings even so. Not only have these strategies floundered in the post-9/11 rhetoric and actions of the Bush administration, they look to me to have been outlawed by two recent federal documents: the 2002 National Security Strategy for the United States and the 107th Congress's Patriot Act. Had I been invited to proofread these puffed-up rhetorical works with the same critical eye I am paid to apply to student rough drafts, I'd have been forced to tell their authors that they had composed two half-truth-telling, hypocrisy-laden pieces of sociopathic cant and that they should throw them away and start over. Both works redefine Earth as a heavenly body whose countries and cultures the Bush administration and Congress were appointed to judge and police. Both are based on the belief that opposing Bush rhetoric is traitorous, that spying on neighbors and friends is patriotic, that fighting for our personal freedom "obstructs enhanced surveillance procedures," that weapons of destruction are our greatest protection against weapons of destruction, that terrorizing the citizens of other nations is the greatest safeguard against terrorist acts against our own nation, that biological health, a sustainable natural economy, and the conservation of ecosystems are beneath consideration in this time of red, white, and blue crisis, and that a daily life of compassion and self-examination is the naive position of sentimentalists and weaklings.

In such an America the teaching of creative writing is one of countless professions that has been inadvertently redefined as dissident. This puts me in an odd position. Having signed a contract to teach before the new Bush/Cheney/Powell "America" existed, and knowing only the former America's literary methods, I'm left no choice but to instruct my students in how to become what the new national lexicon might call "better un-Americans."

II.

Another example of how literature has been forced into a dissident position is Bush's presumption (stated in the 2002 National Security Strategy on page 5) that America's "clear responsibility to history" is to "rid the world of evil." As a lifelong student of the world's Wisdom literature, it is my duty to inform students that "ridding the world of evil" is a goal very different from any recommended by Jesus, Buddha, or Muhammad, though not so different from some recommended by the Josephs Stalin and McCarthy and by Mao Tse-tung. In Wisdom literature the principal evil to be attacked by the person of faith is the evil in oneself, and a secondary evil to be opposed is the power of anyone who victimizes the weak. The 2002 National Security Strategy, on the other hand, is a call for unquestioning obedience to and financial support of the Bush administration's desire to commit our bodies, minds, ravaged ecosystems, workforce, and soldiers to an unspecified series of international bullying actions. Regardless of what we think of this as "patriots," those of us who maintain a politically unfashionable love for the world's scriptures can't help but notice that this document is a hell of a step down in the canon of literature by which people of faith direct their lives.

Another bone I must pick with Bush's aim to "rid the world of evil" is with its authorship. As a novelist, I daily concoct speeches destined to emerge from the mouths of fictitious characters. This practice compels me to point out that every time he speaks formally (which is to say, reads), the president is a fictitious construct pretending to think thoughts placed in his mouth by others. Thus we see, for example, Bush confusing the words "region" and "regime" as he stands before the United Nations pretending to think thoughts that necessitate war. I'm not making fun of these stumbles. It must be hard to enunciate or understand a daily stream of words you have not written, creatively struggled with, or reflected upon prior to pretending, with the world watching, to think them. The good thing about this lack of authenticity is that Bush may not be such as fool as to believe he can "rid the world of evil"; the horrific thing about it is that U.S. military might and foreign policy are being deployed as if he can. This massive pretense does not imply that Bush is a liar. It implies, far more seriously, that the presidency itself has become a pretense, hence a lie.

This brings me back to the impossibility of teaching creative writing under the pretentious new National Security Strategy without seeming dissident. As a voluntary professional fiction writer and involuntary amateur liar, I'm here to tell you that fiction making and lying are two different things. To write *War and Peace* required imaginative effort. To embezzle money from a bank does, too. It should not be necessary to explain even to Jesse Helms that this does not make Tolstoy a bank robber. *War and Peace* is an imaginative invention but also, from beginning to end, a truth telling and a gift giving. We know before reading a sentence that Tolstoy "made it all up," but this making is as altruistic and disciplined as the engineering of a cathedral. It uses mastery of language, spectacular acts of empathy, and meticulous insight into a web of individuals and a world to present a man's vast, haunted love for his Russian people. And we as readers get to recreate this love in ourselves. We get to reenter the cathedral.

A lie is also an imaginative invention, but only on the part of the liar. In hearing a lie we can't share in its creativity. Only the liar knows he's lying. The only "gift" a lie therefore gives anyone is belief in something that doesn't exist. This is the cruelty of all lies. There is no corresponding cruelty in fiction. To lie is to place upon the tongue, page, or TV screen words designed to suppress or distort the truth, usually for the sake of some self-serving agenda.

I fear the Bush administration's claim that Iraq must be attacked, defeated, and occupied for America's domestic safety is just such a distortion, and that its self-serving aim is the embezzlement not of money directly, but of Iraq's oil reserves—the third largest on earth. I hope to heaven I'm wrong, but the $73 million Dick Cheney's cohorts at Halliburton have recently invested in oil infrastructure in Iraq despite the presence of Saddam casts a hell of a shadow over my hope, as do the words of Senator Richard Lugar (R, Indiana) of the Senate Foreign Relations Committee, who during the July/August 2002 hearings on Iraq said, "We are going to run the oil business, we are going to run it well, we are going to make money, and it's going to help pay for the rehabilitation of Iraq because there is money there!"

III.

The Bush/Cheney/Powell Security Strategy and Congressional Patriot Act present us with a daily choice between "unpatriotically" serving living beings, the earth, and international goodwill or "patriotically" serving the corporate nation-state as it transforms our military into a global police force, the world into a police state, and Iraq into an oil-producing colony for "us" and internment camp for its own people. Post-9/11 anti-Saddam talk has usurped thought, annihilated international trust, and polarized our populace. It has endangered Americans abroad and at home. It has led us further and further from reason, history, and physical reality.

Iraq is not Saddam Hussein. It is the cradle of civilization between the Tigris and Euphrates Rivers, home of the Sumerians and ancient Babylonia, of *The Epic of Gilgamesh*, of Bedouin tribes. Iraq is Mesopotamia for Christ's sake, and the estimated 944,000 cigar-sized depleted-uranium-coated bullets we fired and abandoned there during the Gulf War will remain radioactive roughly one million times longer than all the centuries since ancient Mesopotamia was born. Leukemia and other cancers have ballooned since DU arrived. Military spokespersons scoff the coincidence, claiming that DU radiation can be blocked by a sheet of paper. I know of no man, woman, or child with a sheet of paper located between their mouth and stomach or between their nostrils and lungs.

Iraq is not Saddam. It is twenty-two million egregiously sanctioned people, 55 percent of whom now live in poverty, with a growing majority of children now unschooled because of societal breakdown. Millions of Iraqis are chronically malnourished—a condition permanently damaging to children. U.S. pundits who've never seen Iraq praise the U.N. Oil for Food program as the solution to this problem and blame the ever-handy Saddam for the program's failures. But two successive Oil for Food head coordinators, Denis Halliday and Hans von Sponeck, resigned in protest over the program's insufficiencies and now travel the world preaching that malnutrition remains rampant, and that U.S. political manipulation of the sanctions is the greatest cause of the humanitarian crisis in Iraq. A word from that troublesome old moralist, Leo Tolstoy, seems to be in order: "I sit on a man's back, choking him and making him carry me, yet assure myself and others that I am very sorry for him and wish to ease his lot by all possible means—except by getting off his back."

IV.

One of our greatest human traits is compassion, which means, literally, "to suffer with another." But this high art is seldom born in an instant as a response to watching the TV "news," or even in response to firsthand experience. More often compassion's seeds are sewn via a preliminary magic known as empathy. And empathy begins with a fictive act:

What would it be like to be that black girl four rows in front of me? a little white girl wonders in school one morning. Her imagination sets to work, creating unwritten fiction. In her mind she becomes the black girl, dons her clothes, accent, skin, joins her friends after school, goes home to her family, lives that life. No firsthand experience is taking place. Nothing "newsworthy" is happening. Yet a white-girl-turned-fictitiously-black is linking skin hue to life, skin hue to choice of friends and neighborhood, skin hue to opportunity and history. Words she used without thinking—African, color, white—feel suddenly different. And when her imaginary game is over they still sound different. Via sheer fiction, empathy enters a human heart.

To be a Christian, a Buddhist, a Muslim, is to immerse oneself in unstinting fiction making. Jesus's words "Love thy neighbor as thyself," to cite a famously ignored example, demand an arduous imaginative act. This deceptively simple line orders me, as I look at you, to imagine that I am seeing not you, but me, and then to treat this imaginative me, alias you, as if you *are* me. And for how long? Till the day I die! Jesus orders anyone who's serious about Him to commit the "Neighbor = Me" fiction until they forget for good which of the two of themselves to cheat in a business deal or abandon in a crisis or smart-bomb in a war—at which point their imaginative act, their fiction making, will have turned Christ's bizarre words into a reality and they'll be saying with Mother Teresa, "I see Christ in every woman and man."

True, the ability to love neighbor as self is beyond the reach of most people. But the attempt to imagine thy neighbor as thyself is the daily work of every literary writer and reader I know. Literature's sometimes troubling, sometimes hilarious depictions of those annoying buffoons, our neighbors, may be the greatest gift we writers give the world when they become warm-up exercises for the leap toward actually loving our neighbors. Ernest Hemingway's is the definitive statement about this. "Make it up so truly," he said, "that later it will happen that way." This, I dare say, is Christ-like advice, not just to those practicing the artform know as fiction writing, but to anyone trying to live a faith, defend the weak, or sustain this world through love.

V.

It is my best guess, this fifteenth day of November 2002, that the civic grief I'm feeling and words I'm setting down will change nothing in the visible world. Americans in power, through a torrent of anti-literature, have turned twenty-two million of our Iraqi neighbors into a single psychopathic monster. Though I pray I'm wrong and thank the international community for opposing the will of Bush/Cheney/Powell, I still fear that the U.S. may go to war soon, that this war will be brief but devastating, that thousands of children and civilians will die, that we will never be told the number of dead, just as we were not told the numbers killed in Afghanistan or in the Gulf War, and that many Americans for this reason will pretend that no such thousands of dead exist. I fear that weapons of mass destruction will be discovered in Iraq, that this discovery will be hailed as the greatest victory yet in the war against terror, and that the U.S. will use this victory to justify occupying Iraq with a military force whose job it will be to cultivate goodwill and protect us here at home by brandishing weapons of destruction all day every day at Muslims forbidden to brandish their own. I fear that as we shed more red liquid to ensure a flow of black liquid back to the United States we will go on fighting for "homeland security," as we have for three years, by cutting funding to Superfund sites, prying open protected lands to industry, hamstringing laws created to protect vanishing species, reducing safeguards against pollutants, defying the Kyoto Accords, assisting in the corporate copyrighting of Earth's plant and animal species and of America's fresh water, curtailing civil liberties, diverting money from education and human resources to the military, excluding biologists, ecologists, humanitarians, and other voices of compassion and science from policy-making groups ruled by private business and greed, stonewalling clean energy tax breaks and legislation, and ignoring sustainable energy technologies that could prevent future oil wars. I fear these courses of action will lead to ever greater addiction to oil, ever more vicious foreign policy, ever more military actions, hence an ever-more-burning desire on the part of the world's disenfranchised to commit acts of violence against us. I pray no such acts occur, though they already have. I pray the next such act will not involve biochemical or nuclear weapons, though we lead the world in the ownership of both. I pray, I pray, I pray. But the only way I know to pluck from the hearts of enemies their desire to destroy us is to remove from their lives the sense that, for their own physical and spiritual survival, they must.

This work will require tens of thousands of acts of

atonement. Attempting one such act myself, I last year published two essays expressing my incredulity and grief over the U.S. 1992 destruction of Iraq's 1,400 water supply and sewage treatment plants. This destruction took place in defiance of the Geneva Conventions. Worse still, our Defense Intelligence Agency (DIA) predicted in 1991 documents declassified in 2001 that the destruction of these systems would probably not harm Saddam and his army, but would lead to epidemic disease, especially among children. The documents go into surprising detail: they note that Iraq's rivers contain biota and pollutants which, unless treated with chlorine, cause cholera, hepatitis, typhoid, and other diseases. They warn that chlorine was embargoed by the sanctions, as were medicines that treat such diseases. Knowing all this, the G. H. W. Bush administration destroyed Iraq's clean water anyway. Three hundred thousand tons of raw sewage began to flow daily into Iraq's rivers. The sanctions on chlorine and medicine remained in place.

Under the Clinton administration, the DIA documents continued: they mentioned epidemic outbreaks of acute diarrhea, dysentery, respiratory ailments, measles, diphtheria, meningitis, and hepatitis B, causing problems—most notably death—in children. They describe a refugee camp in which four-fifths of the population came down with such diseases: 80 percent of the resulting dead were children. When a team of Harvard physicians witnessed the epidemics in the mid-1990s and urged that sanctions barring medicine be lifted, the DIA said the Iraqi regime was exaggerating the incidence of disease and death for political purposes.

This argument against mercy remains in place to this day. A now-world-famous UNICEF study estimates that 500,000 Iraqi children age five and under have died as a result of the combination of sanctions and defiled water.

VI.

By the time I found and cited the UNICEF study I knew that many Americans had written it off as flawed. I therefore set out, with the help of an Internet-deft, altruistic (and Republican) scholar, to research the pros and cons of the study. I learned that the debate over the "500,000" number is the result of understandable confusion: the same number comes from two different sources.

The first source was a five-day, Iraq-controlled 1995 study of 693 households in Baghdad alone—a study so shoddy that its conclusions were later withdrawn by its own authors. Its estimate of half a million "excess child deaths" due to U.N. sanctions became famous anyway, thanks to a 1996 Leslie Stahl *60 Minutes* interview of then-Secretary of State Madeleine Albright. When Stahl mentioned the flawed study's "500,000 dead," then asked Albright if the sanctions were still worth it, Albright made the double mistake of responding as if the number was fact, and of answering yes. The number was then pounced upon and often exaggerated by humanitarians, inspiring what one might call "counter-humanitarians" to claim in magazines as diverse as *The New Republic*, *Commonweal*, and *National Review* that the number is "in dispute" or "leftist whining," and that all blame for the deaths, whatever the number, should by placed not on the sanctions but on Saddam.

There are two problems with these counterclaims. The first is that, regardless of the precise number of dead, it was the first Bush adminstration, not Saddam's regime, that blew up Iraq's water treatment facilities, and not as an act of war but as a carefully researched act that accurately predicted the ravaging of civilians and children. The second problem with the counterclaims is that the second source of the

"500,000 dead rumor" is no rumor at all: it is the rigorous 1999 child mortality study done by UNICEF.

Based on interviews conducted in 40,000 Iraqi households (with local assistance but conducted with UNICEF involvement at every stage, and with technical support from the World Health Organization and independent analysts) this study too concludes—coincidentally, hence confusingly—that 500,000 more Iraqi children than would have otherwise died in the '90s, died before reaching the age of five as a result of unsafe water.

To greet this finding with politically motivated denials requires an ostrich-length neck and a lot of deep soft sand. The report has been dissected repeatedly. The best such analysis I've found, done by Richard Garfield in 1999, pares away numbers arrived at by shaky data but still concludes that between '91 and '98 there was a "likely sum . . . of 350,000 excess five-and-under child deaths" in Iraq, that these deaths are "the tip of the iceberg among damages" yet to occur, that this disaster far exceeds any level of "acceptable damages according to the principles (of) warfare," and that "sanctions regulations should be modified immediately."

When I first read the UNICEF study my wife and I happened to be nursing our daughters through illnesses that without antibiotics could have killed them both. The number 500,000 destroyed me. The number 350,000 has not brought relief. When I am deeply troubled I fall back on a few trusted mentors. An Indian mentor named Eruch once said, "If you don't know how to take something, take it on the physical level." The closest I can come to following this advice, with regard to the plight of Iraq's children, is to rely on the physical senses, eyes, and heart of a woman named Gerri Haynes.

VII.

Gerri is a Woodinville, Washington, nurse who heads a group called Washington Physicians for Social Responsibility. She had already been on three missions of mercy to Iraq when, after reading my *Orion* online essay, "A Prayer for Water and Children," she invited me to join her on a fourth mission in May of 2002. She was not good at selling her proposal. "It will be sad," she promised. I was unable to join her, in part due to previous commitments, in part due to pure fear. But in September 2002 I telephoned Gerri, and we talked for hours about her four journeys.

The first thing that struck me about Gerri Haynes is how respectful she is toward those who've not been hearing about the kinds of things she has seen. "The psyche wants balance," she told me. "It doesn't want a sudden shocking awareness of things that would compel us to change our lives. In Iraq, children we saw everywhere had the distended bellies of the chronically malnourished. Twelve-year-olds looked like eight-year-olds. . . . An already burdened person can hardly bear (such) news. Most Americans are kind-hearted. The plain sight of suffering and dying children would inspire almost any of them to realign their lives, change their work, their habits, their thinking, anything, if they saw they were contributing to thousands of children's demise. It's very very hard to hear this kind of thing."

I told Gerri that in the face of such nightmares I try to console myself with the fact that I am not the "We" who commits military or foreign policy atrocities. Very quietly, Gerri replied, "But we pay taxes. So we fund these disasters. And it's a bipartisan effort. The Clinton administration was terrible about this, too. This is a government run in both parties by greed and multinational interests, a government that wants nothing to do with true humanitarian aims. Human beings are all made of the same delicate fabric. That's where my 'We' comes from."

My small consolation vanished.

We spoke of the 1999 UNICEF child mortality studies. Gerri's take: "The numbers vary widely, from somewhere around 300,000 to a high of maybe two million. Physicians in Baghdad, when I was there in '99, estimated that 100 to 150 kids were dying just there, every day. But it's a number that's impossible to prove for several reasons. One is that the mechanisms Iraqis had for gathering statistics have not been put back together since the Gulf War. Another is that, after it became apparent that there were limited drugs in the hospitals, many Iraqis stopped bringing their very sick children in. This was particularly true in Basra, where there's a large Bedouin population. These people just keep their kids home, and bury them at home. Gathering exact statistics is impossible.

"We do know that the level of leukemia is greatly increased. We know that congenital malformation has greatly increased. In May 2002 we talked with a woman scientist, Souad Al Azzawi, who said that if the rise in leukemia had been due, as some U.S. politicians claim, to burning oil fires, the pollutants that have since cleared from the environment would have caused the number of leukemia cases to come down. Instead, leukemia levels began to rise five to seven years after 1991—the expected time frame following radiation exposure—and have remained inordinately high. Many believe the answer is DU."

I was impressed that Gerri did not accuse. She just said "many believe."

"But this doesn't say anything," she added, "to the experience of going to hospital after hospital and seeing every bed with a child in it, sometimes two childen per bed—children that look to my eye as though they're very close to death. It doesn't speak to the experience of watching mothers and fathers feel hopeless and helpless to save their children. We live on hope. How can we not tell other Americans about what we have participated in creating?"

In 2000, shortly before a planned fourth trip to Iraq, Gerri Haynes was diagnosed with breast cancer. When she mentioned this during my interview of her, I was already so undone by all she'd been saying that I lacked the good grace to ask what she'd been through, or what her prognosis was. I only know that, whatever she endured that year, in September 2001 she was prepared to lead another humanitarian group to Iraq.

Then 9/11 happened. Gerri said, "The delegation had to wait for travel to again become possible. Then they had to try to reorganize. It was difficult. It's very expensive to go there. And time-consuming for people who have full-time jobs—people who are using their vacation time to do this arduous, upsetting work."

But in May 2002, Gerri returned to Iraq yet again.

Before this recent trip—amid all the American flag waving and war rumblings—Gerri's oldest daughter tried to persuade her to stay home. Gerri didn't describe their discussion, but she did say that, after finally accepting Gerri's sense of mission, daughter offered mother an old-souled piece of advice. "If you do go," she said, "be completely present, wherever you go."

These words returned to Gerri in May 2002, in an Iraqi hospital virtually bereft of medicine and hope. While her group moved from bed to bed, Gerri approached a woman sitting next to her dying child. Gerri speaks no Arabic. The woman spoke no English. Trying to be "present" anyway,

Gerri looked at the child, then at the mother, and placed her right hand over her own heart.

The Iraqi mother placed her right hand over her own heart.

Gerri's eyes and the mother's eyes simultaneously filled with tears.

The hospital was crowded. Gerri's visitation time was short. She started to move to the next bed, but then remembered her daughter's words: "completely present." She and the mother were already crying, their hands over their hearts. There was nothing Gerri could do, despite her medical training, for the child. "How much more present," she wondered, "is it possible to be?"

She stepped forward anyway. With no plan but vague allegiance to the commandment, "completely present," the nurse without medicine stepped toward the bed of the dying child and inconsolable mother. She then put both of her hands out, palms up.

The Iraqi mother fell into her arms.

"If only this experience were unique!" Gerri told me. "But I can't tell you, any longer, how many mothers I've now held in this same way."

Her voice grew faint over the phone.

I heard: "...diseases that children would almost never die from in the U.S...."

I heard: "...medicine so basic..."

Then her voice faded, or maybe I drowned it out. I've never taken interview notes while sobbing before.

VIII.

In 1967, at the height of the Vietnam War, Dr. Martin Luther King Jr. may have felt like a minority of one when he spoke up, at the Riverside Church in New York City, against the flag wavers and public opinion polls of the day. He still had the courage to say, "A time comes when silence is betrayal. Men do not easily assume the task of opposing their government's policy, especially in time of war. We must speak with all the humility that is appropriate to our limited vision, but we must speak. For we are deeply in need of a new way beyond the darkness so close around us.... We are called upon to speak for the weak, for the voiceless, for the victims of our nation, for those it calls enemy, for no document from human hands can make these humans any less our brothers."

To abandon the words of Dr. King is to let the bullet kill him a second time.

I believe, based on his call, that no matter what happens in the coming war with Iraq, we lose. We lose because we already lost. We lost in our first effort there when we flew 110,000 sorties over Iraq in forty-two days, dropping 88,500 tons of ordnance, more than in all of World War II, on an unsortable tangle of military installations, palaces, power plants, communications sites, mosques, schools, homes, civilians, soldiers in arms, soldiers in retreat, soldiers in postures of surrender, soldiers too shell-shocked to do anything but stand in the road and accept annihilation. We lost when we characterized our slaughter of the retreating Iraqi army as a "turkey shoot" and the incinerated bodies of fathers and sons as "crispy critters." We lost when Colin Powell, asked for the number of Iraqi dead produced by this blitzkrieg, responded, "Frankly that's a number that doesn't interest me very much." We lost when the first Bush administration researched the destruction of water systems, read predictions of death to children, and destroyed the systems anyway. We lost when we urged the

U.N. to ban chlorine and medicines, witnessed the ensu-
ing epidemics, and refused to ease the sanctions. We lost
when we scattered tons of depleted uranium dust over Iraq
that will go on assaulting all life-forms for eons. We lost
when we were apprized of studies showing such cancer
increases as lymphoma (fourfold), lung (fivefold), breast
(sixfold), uterine (nearly tenfold), skin (elevenfold), liver
(elevenfold), ovarian (sixteenfold), but still denied the connection, still make and deploy DU, and recently nixed, by
pressuring the U.N., a World Health Organization study
of DU in Iraq. We lost when we allocated $355.5 billion
toward more such "defense" activities in 2003. We will go
on losing as long as we go on pretending to prevent evil by
inflicting these abysmal "strategies."

There is no man or woman, no nation, no mortal power
on earth capable of "ridding the world of evil" as George W.
Bush has vowed to do. The desire is preposterous. To act
upon preposterousness with vast military might is evil. To
acquiesce in such evil is somnolence.

One billion two hundred and fifty million Muslims share
this world with us. Bush/Cheney/Powell seem to seek their
mass conversion to American corporate "values." I seek, in
the face of my own or anyone's failure to live by the gospels
or Koran, to "make it up so truly that later it will happen
that way." I seek to make up, then live, Dr. King's sense of
brotherhood and Nurse Haynes's sense of sisterhood with
people who surrender five times a day "to the Merciful, the
Compassionate."

To define compassion as dissident does not alter the
Compassionate. To define mercy as unpatriotic or nonstra-
tegic does not change the eternally Merciful. Gerri Haynes
placing her palms out to the mother of a dying child, that

mother falling into her arms, their joined tears—*this* is a victory over evil.

The child died even so.

Jesus. Muhammad. Allah. God. Help our "strategists" and "patriots" make up our neighbors more truly.

5

• • • • • • • •

Ashes & Dirt

In October 2003 I was invited to give a one-hour talk in Seattle to a churchful of people gathered in honor of St. Francis of Assisi on his feast day. I was asked to direct a few remarks, if so moved, toward our proper human relationship with the earth, since Francis is held to exemplify such a relationship. I had one work day to prepare. When I spent that day attempting to set down a few honest words about just what sort of earth or nature lover the man from Assisi really was, I suffered total literary failure. Faced, at day's end, with *no* time to describe St. Francis, I was left with no choice but to describe my failure to describe St. Francis. Thus did I get to live, rather than just write, the fact that if there's anything I've learned from Francis of Assisi it is that failure, spiritually speaking, is far more edifying than success.

This particular failure began with research and notes. I noted, for instance, that the man in whose honor we had gathered was not really named Francis: he was named John by his parents, Peter and Pica Bernadone of Assisi, but Peter spent so much time on the road enriching his already rich self that he was off trading in France when his son was born, causing mischievous neighbors to nick the baby's name to *Francesco*, which basically means: "the French Guy."

I researched the saint online and found some distressingly cuddly websites that call Francesco stuff like "the Father of the Ecology Movement." I couldn't see this. For all his love of nature, Francis was consumed by his love for Jesus, and to link such a love to the Sierra Club or Audubon Society is drivel. Francis was neither an activist nor a contemplative, as I see him: he was some kind of molten force capable of conducting his outer life at full speed without his self-conflagration of an inner life getting lost or even dimmed for an instant.

He was also, I duly noted, a nonintellectual and a terrible literalist. To wit:

Because Jesus said *Give everything to the poor and follow me*, Francis gave away his home, his parents, his dignity, his lute, his hat with the cool feather, and every stitch of clothes, till he stood naked as a baby in the middle of downtown with the whole city watching. And because Genesis said that God made and blessed all creatures, plants, landforms, and elements, Francis loved them all, including wolves, lizards, snakes, blizzards, volcanoes, rain and lightning storms, and every creepy crawly biting stinging insect, plant, or human, especially those that attacked, and so in his view "blessed," the person of Francis himself. And because the Son of Man had no place to lay His head, Francis refused to own a bed, home, winter cloak, or even sandals to negotiate the stone terrain of Umbria, and so spent his life bare and bloody-footed, which is again to say "blessed," by a billion stones.

What most of us might consider our "imaginative" or "prayer" or "inner" lives Francis considered his vivid, immediate, physical life. The visible body of his boon companion, Jesus, for instance, left this world some twelve hundred years before Francis was even born, reducing lesser men and women to a relationship consisting chiefly of prayer, hymns, old Bible stories, or the waging of wars in His Name. Francis, however, not only prayed and sang to and told stories about Jesus, he talked with and danced for and bowed and babbled to Him, animatedly, constantly, like no one we see nowadays but the streetmad or bag ladies—Christ-crazed Francis thanking his unseen Pal for every blow received at the hands of thugs, every pang of hunger, every insult from skeptics and mockers, every turn of the weather (especially for the ever-blessèd worse), every scrap of begged food (especially the rancid, the maggoted, the moldy).

But even Francis had a body. And in and of itself this body was a trembling, comfort-loving animal, like my own. And there were times in his long marriage to Poverty when this body hadn't eaten in days, or even weeks, and was literally starving, so that when Francis or his brothers finally begged a little food, and once in a blue moon got to cook it, the smells that arose were so rare and marvelous that, upon bowing over the food, even in Christ's Presence, Francis's eyes would water and his saliva would spurt and he would crave that food not only because it was the gift of God but because *dang*, it smelled *great!*, and his poor little body was stark-raving *starvin'!*

Any "ecologist" I know, in such straits, would thank Earth for her bounty and devour the food with utmost animal happiness. Not so our Assisian. When this kind of anticipation rose up in Francis, his heart stopped him on a dime, *errt!*, stood him up, and sent him to the nearest stove or campfire, where he'd grab a fistful of ashes, return to his lovely food, and sling the ashes on. In every year of

Our Lord since this killjoy condiment was self-applied by Francis, we his fans have asked, sometimes with our mouths full, sometimes on his feast day: *Why o why o why?*

Perhaps, I would dare guess, because food topped with ashes is exceedingly hard for the mind or body to desire, and "*desirelessness,*" said the excommunicated saint Meister Eckhart, "*is the virgin who eternally gives birth to the Son.*" Having preserved this virginity and birth with ashes—having forced even his *body* to pray when it tasted the wrecked meal and exclaimed, "Jesus *Christ*, Francis!"—the French Guy lit into his meal with gooey, gray-mouthed relish.

As I studied on all this I felt awe, for a while. But as my notes grew into paragraphs and Francis's Christ-loving deeds multiplied and the desperation of deed only deepened, it finally occurred to me—in the animal comfort of my study, clothing, warm socks, and stone-defying shoes—that to give a man as average as me a chance to speak of a man as sublimely love-crazed as Francis is to give that average man a chance to sound like a high-flown, pious ninny. Francis's love for his Lord was so ecstatic, creative, and physical that, even though there are things I believe I would die for, I feel, in comparison to this man, that I have hardly begun to love anyone or anything at all. Francis, as far as I can see, had no "average" or "ecological" or "everyday" sense of this life: for him every creature was a miracle, every moment a gift, every breath a prayer in Christ's Presence, and if we were sitting with Francis tonight, disbelieving his senses of miracle, gift, and Presence completely, he'd go on believing in them so much more joyously and contagiously than we bums know how to disbelieve that our only escape from the transformational conflagration of his love would be to flee the room.

Feeling all this as I looked over my little Feast Day paragraphs, I suddenly felt so papery, so uncomfortably comfortable, so lamely literary and unbearably abstract, that I did something bag-lady strange: with all the love for the French Guy I could muster, I abandoned my computer and office, marched to the kitchen, grabbed a teaspoon, took it in the living room, opened the woodstove, dug out a heaping teaspoonful of cold ashes, and—hoping to learn at least the flavor, if not the feeling, that Francis knew so well—shoved them in my mouth.

Guess what?

I got two more paragraphs out of it.

Paragraph One

The taste wasn't as shocking as I'd feared—at first. Woodstove ashes taste the same way they smell—at first. But the mouth encloses this taste so completely, and your taste buds and salivary glands then greet it so confusedly, that the encounter intensifies, soon taking you places well beyond anything you could detect from the smell. Ashes taste, after you've worked them around in your mouth a while, like a message from somewhere far beyond this life. The literary part of me wants to say something like, *"Ashes taste like the most incinerated piece of sixth-circle-of-hell bowge-meat Dante ever imagined!"* But ashes, in truth, taste like something well beyond the literary part of me. My writings and life have somehow made me the half-honored, half-heartbroken recipient of tiny vials of the ashes of four valiant young boys. I have many beloved friends and family who are ashes today, too. I began to taste them. Yet this taste, strange to say, did not sadden me. If I were to assign a single word to the flavor in my mouth I'd say it was that of *finality*. But finality, in turn, has much in common with eternity, and what eternity is to time, infinity is to space, and as the great Indian gospel, the *Upanishads*, put it and Francis truly lived it: *There is no joy in the finite. There is joy only in the Infinite.* This, I suddenly saw, was why Francis threw his gray condiment on every alluring morsel and animal pleasure in his path: the opposite of a killjoy, he was joy's greatest lover, choosing, each time he trashed his food, a life of no joy but Infinite soul-joy. *"An equation way beyond you!"* my ego quickly, nervously warned. Yet, next thing you know, I was tasting a Beginning hidden in the Harsh End in my mouth, and felt joy rising not in spite of, but *because* of, the spoonful of finality/dead boys/dead friends/eternity/infinity in there.

Paragraph Two:

But woodstove ashes come in extremely dry, powdery form. And the taste of hidden Beginning was so unexpected and sweet that I drew a sharp breath of surprise—*hnhhh!?*—and so inhaled a cloud of ash and commenced to cough my lungs out. I spent the next good while at the bathroom sink, discovering that it's remarkably hard to wash the deep gray color of Finality Flavor off your tongue. I also registered a stomachache for reasons I hope the chemists in the crowd will keep to themselves.

Those are my two paragraphs. That was my literary failure. I was out of time, and had no idea what to tell the good people who would gather in Francis's honor the next day in Seattle. But a story isn't necessarily over because the writer of the story thinks it's over ...

Having intentionally sampled and unintentionally inhaled the only spoonful of ashes I have ever imbibed, I strolled—stomachache, residual joy, gray spit, hacking cough, and all—the quarter mile out to my mailbox, where I happened to find an envelope from my friend, the Portland essayist Brian Doyle. The page inside the envelope did not, however, turn out to be by Brian: all he'd done was place an exclamation point atop a letter he'd just received from Japan. Here that letter is, verbatim:

!

Dear Mr. Brian Doyle:

My name is Aya Okada and I work for company called "Formulation." We produce television programs for . . . one of biggest networks in Japan. Currently, (we) are planning . . . a program that will mention physical secrets of Human-beings. . . . In this program we will show the people who eats dirt. Which is why we decided to ask for your help. I have read your report about your sons. I would like to ask you about some questions, shown below.

-When did your children start eating dirt?
-Do they eat dirt now?
-How much do they usually eat?
-How old are they?
-Are there bad influence from eating dirt?
-Could you and your sons accept for our interview about eating dirt?

That is the all questions I would like to ask you in this time. I hope hearing from you soon.

Sincerely,
Aya Okada.

As I made my way back to the house, occasionally slowing to hack up a little more gray crud, I considered the sequence of events that had placed this missive in my hands:

+ a journalist in Japan somehow grows curious about dirt eating;
+ she finds a little something on the topic by a writer in far-off America;
+ she writes to the writer, who lives in Portland;
+ this writer, in turn, finds her query so amusing that he sends it to a pal in Montana six hundred miles away, causing a Japanese query into dirt eating to arrive in the Montanan's hand *at the very moment he has, for the first time in fifty-one years of life, indulged in a fit of ash eating.*

I stopped walking and looked suspiciously at the sky. Was I to consider all this "a coincidence"? Or might Francis and his nail-pierced Pal have been looking down on me from On High, throwing elbows, slapping knees, and laughing till the Son of Man wept and the French Guy shot wet stuff out his nose?

Back in the house, my next ashen-mouthed move was to make a phone call.

"Brian!" I barked when my friend answered. "Who the hell is *Aya Okada* and what have you been '*reporting*' to her about your fine sons?"

Two minutes later, thanks to the techno-miracle of e-mail, I was back in my study reading the "report" that caught Ms. Okada's eye. It turned out to be an essayette by Brian that appeared in an American anthology called *Best Spiritual Writing 2000.* Here it is:

Eating Dirt

I have a small daughter and two smaller sons, twins. They are all three in our minuscule garden at the moment, my sons eating dirt as fast as they can get it off the planet and down their gullets. They are two years old, they were seized with dirt-fever an instant ago, and as admirably direct and forceful young men, quick to act, true sons of the West, they are going to *eat some dirt*, boy, and you'd better step aside.

My daughter and I step aside.

The boys are eating so much dirt so fast that much of it is missing their maws and sliding muddily down their chicken chests. . . . I watch a handful as it travels. It's rich brown stuff, almost black, crumbly. In a moment I will pull the boy over and issue a ticket, but right now I watch with interest as he inserts the dirt, chews meditatively, emits a wriggling worm, stares at it—and eats it, too.

"Dad, they're eating *the garden*," says my daughter.

So they are and I'll stop them, soon. But for this rare minute in life . . . I feel, inarticulately, that there's something simple and true going on here. Because we all eat dirt. Fruits and vegetables are dirt transformed by light and water. Animals are vigorous dirt, having dined on fruit, vegetables or other animals who are dirt. Our houses and schools and offices are cupped by dirt and made of wood, stone and brick—former dirt. Glass is largely melted sand, a kind of clean dirt. Our clothing used to be dirt. Paper was trees was dirt. . . . We breathe dirt suspended in the air, crunch it between our teeth on spinach leaves . . . , wear it in the lines of our hands and folds of our faces, catch it in . . . our noses, eyes, ears. Some people are driven by private fires to eat dirt—a condition called *pica* [the name of Francis the Ash-eater's mother!], from the Latin word for magpie—a bird with no culinary objection to dirt, dogdoo, carrion. We swim in an ocean of regular normal orthodox there-it-sits-under-everything dirt.

The children tire, sun retreats, in we go to wash the garden off my sons. It swirls down the bath-drain, into the river, eventually to the ocean . . . ends up as silt . . . sinks to the ocean floor . . . becomes kelp, razor clams, sea otters . . . rises, is drawn up into rain, and returns to our garden after its un-imaginable vacation.

My daughter and I discuss these journeys. And when the rain begins we draw a map—which we leave on the back porch—so our dirt will know how to come home to our house.

"Maybe there are dirt fairies," says my daughter. "Or maybe the dirt can read."

Maybe my daughter is right. Consider this essay, made by dirt worked in wondrous ways into bone, blood, protein, water, synaptic electricity and words. So why couldn't dirt read *and* write? Why couldn't dirt lean against a fence with smaller lovelier dirt in his lap, and watch twin dirt demons devour dirt while the world spins in its miraculous mysterious circles, ashes to ashes, dust to dust, without end?

End of Brian's meditation. End of my attempt to fathom the fathomless Assisian in ink upon paper. End of my fail-ure to capture anything for a Seattle audience but a mouthful of gray goo and the strange story of my day. But there will never be an end to Francis's and your and my and every present and departed earthling's relationship with the mystery, finality, and transformative infinity of there-they-lie-under-everything ashes and dirt. And my gray tongue and I taste, in this hard but mysterious fact, a paradoxical yet undeniable hint of joy.

6

Christian Matters I

a Scanner *magazine conversation with*
Craig van Rooyen, conducted in 1998,
excised & edited for this book by DJD

Scanner: What was your early connection to Adventism?

DJD: I had no personal, felt connection to Seventh-day Adventism. I had an impersonal, matriarch-engineered connection. The matriarch of my family was my grandmother, Ethel Rowe. Historically, let's see, I guess it was her grandfather, James Rowe, who engineered the family connection to Adventists. He was part of the SDA community at Walla Walla, Washington.

My grandma Ethel—who was like a second mother to us—was raised in more or less Adventist logging camps around Trout Lake, Washington. Gramma Rowe epitomizes my early connection to the church. She was a wonderful woman in many ways—a dynamo, really, full of faith and zeal and energy. She came from a family so poor that she dropped out of school in the second grade in order to earn money, and left home for good at age twelve, to become a house cleaner in Vancouver, Washington, and later a beautician in Portland. Gramma Rowe was smart, feisty as hell, faith-driven, and very loving toward us—though her love was the kind that sometimes made you wish she felt indifferent. She worked like a maniac, having come from such poverty, so the only additional education she got after second grade was real estate school. As a result, she taught my siblings and me to worship and pray in a second-grade way, and think about Jesus in a second-grade way. And the naive and loving part of this was a good thing. No way into the kingdom "except as children," right? But her brand of religion also included the judgmentalism, tantrums, self-righteousness, racial prejudice, shallowness, and material-ism of a second grader. A naughty second grader at that!

So, like so many fundamentalist or Catholic kids, I felt both cursed and loved by my religious family members, and was simultaneously attracted to and repelled by their half-loving, half-hating faith.

Scanner: What are your early memories of being Adventist? Did you eat veggie links, memorize verses, read *Uncle Arthur's Bedtime Stories*, and refrain from playing baseball on Sabbath?

DJD: Before I delve into my lifelong churchophobia, I want to provide readers with a sort of Warning Label: my own experience is not intended to be an example to *anybody*. It's just my own experience. *Read your own hearts, everyone! Feel your own feelings!*

That said: my earliest memory of Adventist faith train-ing is of being four years old in Sabbath School and having to sing "Jesus Wants Me for a Sunbeam" while making our fingers extend out around our faces like "sunbeams." I felt nothing for Jesus as we did this—and I loved Jesus; found Him heroic from earliest memory. All I can recall feeling during the sunbeam song, though, was bafflement that our teachers would make us do such silly things.

Similar confusion invaded my attempts to recite "Now I Lay Me Down to Sleep" at bedtime. Not only did this prayer not give me courage to face the night, it felt unfair to say it. To expect God to listen to a rote ditty, then protect us in response, seemed like offering Him almost nothing but asking Him for a lot. As for the time I asked Jesus for a base hit at a ball game, when I stepped to the plate and struck out on three pitches I was relieved: if every kid in America could get a hit just by asking Jesus, we'd all bat a thousand and ruin baseball in a day. I was born, so far as I can remember, with a sense that prayer must be spontaneous and deeply heartfelt in order to be genuine. On the other hand, how do we get through the nonspontaneous, unheartfelt parts of our daily lives? I wrestle with this paradox to this day.

Uncle Arthur stories? I was aware of them but didn't read any. And I was saved from the veggie links by my father, who disliked his Adventist boarding school so much that he forbade what he considered "boarding school" trappings, like vegetarianism, in his home. But the men were primarily "providers" in my family. The women were our religious leaders. And in my grandmother and mother's view we had no option but to "be Adventist and like it," "be Adventist or be damned"—cheery formulas of that good old-fashioned sort!

Scanner: Your family left the Adventist church one by one over the years, ending with your mother's recent departure. What are the stories of this group exodus?

DJD: Those stories, in their meaningful depth, are so personal to each of my family members than I've no right to tell them. I can tell you that my brother John left the church first, at seventeen, via death. A series of heart surgeries that didn't work. Because he put up a hell of a fight, it took him a year to die, and my family spent that year praying for an opposite result. So his death had a powerful effect on all of us. But I've told my own share of that story too many times. The statute of limitations has run out. And what the rest of my family went through is theirs to tell.

My brother Steve left the Adventists in his late teens. I don't think he'd mind me saying that. If I remember right, the trouble began when an Adventist academy booted him out because his hair touched his glasses in the front. Steve is a born Bible scholar. If the Bible had said that hair shouldn't touch glasses in the front, then fine, he would obey. But it didn't. So he refused to trim it, got the boot, and went on to earn three advanced degrees from a Baptist seminary, where his contrarianism and scriptural fidelity led him to write a brilliant dissertation on the biblical grounds for polygamy—which didn't exactly thrill his conservative thesis advisors. Entertainingly feisty guy, my brother!

During that same time Steve went back and did scholarly research on the historical beginnings of Adventism. This research convinced him that Adventism is just Protestantism with some quirks tacked on by the avowed "prophetess," Sister Ellen G. White. And it's a funny thing about my family. My mother, grandmother, Santa Cruz sister, conservative big brother, easygoing younger brother, and I unanimously agree on almost nothing. But one thing we've always agreed on is that there is no reason on earth to become followers of Sister Ellen G. White.

Scanner: Why did you personally leave the Adventist faith, or (to paraphrase Yogi Berra) when you came to that fork in the road, how did you take it?

DJD: For me personally, it bugged me that the SDAs were started by a fellow—William Smith, wasn't he called, in about 1844, wasn't it?—who believed he'd studied his Bible so carefully that he'd discovered the day Jesus was coming. Must've been a powerful preacher, Smith, because he convinced a lot of people to leave their farms rotting and join him on a hillside on Second Coming Day. When Jesus didn't show, Smith said he was a year off. When they waited a year and nothing happened again, they had a choice. Tar and feather the son of a bitch, or start a church. I've never understood why they chose the latter. Armageddonists give me the creeps.

But that's only the negative side of the story. The positive side, as I've said many times, is that unmediated, intensely felt spiritual experiences were coming to me often in boyhood. Just not from a church. The faith I was gaining in my Creator was coming from Creation itself. The intricacies and spirit of wild things often felt literally holy to me—whereas my distrust of the intricacies and spirit of churchgoing is as old as my memory. But again: *I'm not trying to be a role model in this.* Go to church if you like it! I don't want to be the Sister David James White of wilderness and fly-fishing! I just want to be spiritually honest with your admirably honest magazine.

Scanner: Did anything about being Adventist feed your sense of wonder?

DJD: Not at church, that I can recall. But I'm tired of my own religious war stories. Complain complain complain! And individual humans who call themselves Adventists have many times fed my sense of wonder—though through their humanness, not their Adventism. My impossible Gramma Rowe, first and foremost. What a terror and hoot she was! Yet after all our ups and downs, she held my sister

Katherine's and my hand for hours as she was dying (though she'd previously disinherited both of us in a religious fury!). And her last words to me, after predicting hellfire for me at least a thousand times, were, "I love you, David." Can't beat that.

Another wonder I've felt from Adventists: since *The Brothers K* came out it has, to my amazement, been read with enthusiasm by large numbers of practicing SDAs, a hundred or more of whom have written me letters that reach past seemingly opposed dogmas and speak heart to heart. These letters have been an enormous gift. Listen to a bit of one from a woman who recently moved to America from Korea, and read *Bros K* to help get a handle on our country:

> *"I feel so sad because so little I could put this feeling of mine into words about your book. . . . This is how one family is built and continues to grow. All these children wanted to run, escape, rebel and search yet they cannot change the fact that this is their family, and they cannot change. . . . If there was no Everett, no Laura's frantic religion, no Peter's search for Buddha, no Grandma's Darwinism, no twins' scientific method, no Irwin's Vietnam pains, no Kincaid's narration and silence and no Hugh's failure in baseball, they are never going to see each other clearly like this way. I think, deep in their each one's heart, they found REAL ONE BEING just like Kincaid's dream of Kingdom of Heaven."*

"REAL ONE BEING!" Amen, my Korean friend!

Scanner: Can you imagine organized religion as a communal expression of spiritual wonder? How would such a church be structured? Or is structure the antithesis of spirituality?

DJD: There have, in many cultures, for thousands of years, been marvelous communal expressions of spiritual wonder. The Adventism of my boyhood lived in ignorance of this. So do most Americans today—fundamentalists and so-called secularists, it would seem, about equally (especially if they watch equal amounts of TV). But the communal expression of spiritual wonder is there to be studied, seen, resurrected, and loved in the cultures, religions, mythologies, and arts of the entire world. It just so happens that you and I—through no fault of our own—were born into a religion that called most such wonders "heathenism" or "devil worship."

Going back to your phrase "communal expression of spiritual wonder," a question I have for any sincere religionist is: why try to extend your vocabulary or your life beyond that lovely phrase? Jesus, the "Adventist" Himself, spent the famous portion of His life moving on foot around a very small part of the world, demonstrating in word and deed that there is no goal beyond the experience and expression of love. If you've got yourself a little faith community and feel some love and mercy bubbling in it, why mess with that? Why "structure" it? Why "enchurch" it? Why not just live it and be thankful?

On the other hand, I too have grandiose "structure" dreams. Though I try to repress it, I've got my prophet side, believe me. I look at Sister White's gnarly old face sometimes and think, "There but for the grace of God go I!" I feel, for instance, that it would be incredibly beneficial to millions of us if our "communal expressions of spiritual wonder" took place in *real* communities. I have spiritual community with scores of individuals, but we're scattered to the winds, and unable, so far, to extricate ourselves from the mainstream techno-industrial monolith. And telecommunity is not community. A wonderful faith community to be part of would not be scattered like this, or dependent on uncontrollable and creepy companions like ExxonMobil, GE, agribusiness, and the Pentagon like this. It wouldn't be you and a few of your pals in Fresno, Naples, Albuquerque, Seattle, and Buffalo, living in 'burbs that look more and more as if Barbie, Mickey Mouse, and Ronald McDonald designed them.

A sustaining spiritual community would be a self-sustaining physical community rooted in its own particular soil and watershed, with its own idiosyncratic expressions of universal spiritual truths. To my mind, such a community might look a bit like an Amish community, physically, if it was rural. But an even better model might be an updated version of the medieval Beguines.

The Beguines—Ellen G. White and Mary Baker Eddy and Joseph Smith and Calvin and Luther followers should know this!—were communities of what I would call "feminist mystics" that rose up in the Rhine Valley before and during the time of my greatest Christian hero, Meister Eckhart, and spread all over Europe. The Beguines had several great leaders—all of them women, all experiential mystics—and many powerful allies in the church, chief among them the incomparable Eckhart. The Beguines had a daily devotional life which was taken very seriously, but differed from the life led by nuns in that they lived comparatively free of the church, and right out there "in the world." Beguine women lived on their own private property, not Roman Church property—which was stupendously freeing for them, and they prospered because of it. Their independence was fierce, but so, in the spirit of Christ, was their generosity. They raised their own food, they educated the local children, they took care of the sick and dying, they took in orphans, and—like Eckhart—they read and unpacked the Bible to everyday people *in their native tongues*, so that the example of Jesus could be understood and emulated by all. Their communities were both self-sustaining *and* woven into the society at large, and they were of huge benefit to society. Yet they were based on experiential mysticism—or, to use your term, "the communal expression of spiritual wonder."

The church of the day, however, the STRUCTURE, was a Rome-based patriarchy uncomfortable with the existence of women at all, let along self-giving, heroic, Christ-adoring women who expressed their spiritual wonder in the striking manner of the great Beguine mystics—or *any* women mystics. Here's Pope Gregory the XIII holding forth on a certain mystic, for example: "*Teresa of Avila . . . is a filthy and immoral nun who is indecent in the highest degree and simply uses her busy efforts . . . as an excuse for indulging in her dissipated lusts.*"

The passion, power, and beneficience generated by the Beguines showed good ol' boys like Pope Greg to be the power-drunk misogynists they were. Which enraged them. So down came the Iron Bible of the Inquisition, *ka-thunk!* The Beguines and Beguinages were crushed mercilessly, their greatest leaders imprisoned or burned at the stake, their brilliant mystical texts and poems and songs of love burned with them, their mercies and loving service revoked, the poor and sick whom they'd served turned back out on the streets, their homeless followers sent to nunneries or ghettos.

The Beguines' teachings and joys were so mercilessly eradicated that I'll bet not one in a thousand modern Adventist women has even heard of them. And this haunts me. I can't help but feel that if women in Europe and the Americas had been encouraged to study and celebrate the lives and

communitarian example of these loving, creative females of
their own Christian tradition—the "filthy and immoral nun"
of Avila, Hadewijch of Brabant, Mechtild of Magdeburg,
and Marguerite Porette (burned at the stake by men for her
beautiful love of God), to name just a few—we may have
gotten a better handle on what my Korean pen pal calls "the
REAL ONE BEING deep in their each one's heart," and so
never have suffered the spiritual vacuum that enabled the
rise of third-rate prophets like Mary Baker Eddy, Ellen G.
White, and Joseph Smith.

The tantalizing possibility here is: look at the American
Indian nations that—despite five hundred years of genocide,
displacement, destruction of languages and lifeways—are
currently doing tremendous things to recreate their spiritual and cultural roots. Look at the resurrection of Irish,
Scottish, Welsh, Breton, Cornish, and Manx languages and
poetry and culture in Europe. Look at the resurgence of interest in the Beguines. And hope your heart out! When you
study the Beguines and Eckhart it hits you that Christianity,
like the Indian nations and indigenous Celtic cultures, has
been violently separated from its own greatest spiritual and
communal riches, and violently constricted, the result being
the unlivable politicized fundamentalism of today. But
Christians, like the Indians, are in a strong position to fight
(nonviolently!) to win these spiritual riches back. In the five
centuries since the destruction of the Beguine communities
and posthumous excommunication of Eckhart, mysticism
has died as a popular force within Christian culture. I believe this loss of mystical vitality goes a long way toward
explaining how Christianity has become so splintered and
politicized, and the rest of the Western world so secularized.
Without applied mysticism and Christ-like giving and living saints and angels and heroic poverty, chastity, and obe-

dience, Christianity becomes rote, heartless, and BORING! People sense this—the idealistic and gifted young, especially, sense it—and leave the faith.

What excites me about this state of affairs is the fact that divine desperation sometimes drives people to acts of great spiritual creativity. And, so far as I can see, there is no longer any Inquisitorial-type institution in place to prevent Beguinages, or something very like them, from forming once again. The tribes' recovery efforts and the Celtic and Breton resurgences show us that the five-hundred-year distance between us and the Beguines is not unbridgeable. Especially not if, as I believe, we have no choice. I feel, I've *always* felt, that American and European women are exceptionally spirited, and that our men become lost, evil, or just dull as hell without them. I'm sexist in this way. I sense that, in the next hundred years or so, Western women are going to do amazing things in terms of "communal expression of spiritual wonder." And Western men and the world will end up in wildly better shape because of it. Our lack of community is intensely painful. A TV talk show is not community. A couple hours in a church pew each Sabbath is not community. A multinational corporation is neither a human nor a community, and in the sweatshops, defiled agribusiness fields, genetic mutation labs, ecological dead zones, the inhumanity is showing. Without genuine spiritual community, life becomes a struggle so lonely and grim that even Hillary Clinton has admitted "it takes a village." I meet a lot of men and women who want to do something about this—but the women tend to be more fired up about it, in part because the best qualities of women are largely banished from the mainstream industrial culture, in part because most women are not so big into beer, chips, and football.

Dang! You never should have asked me "how such a

church could be structured"! But there's something afoot here. Crazy as I may sound to the average *Wall Street Journal* pundit, I travel a lot, and in those travels meet thousands of intelligent Americans who are seriously pondering new ways of forging community and sustainability and expressions of spiritual wonder. The "socially responsible investment" movement is an example. But why not carry it a step further? The communes of the '60s were for the most part a sexist, druggy joke—an adolescent boy's rock-and-roll fantasy. A serious attempt to change our lives on all levels was never truly made. The Beguines, in huge contrast, were a thriving, grounded, love-driven mystical movement that absolutely worked in the urban centers and in the sticks.

I believe they're the Great Forgotten Model. Picture a group of very modest but lovely little structures on four hundred or so acres somewhere, with its own fresh water source, decent enough soil, twenty or so families, plus twenty or so monks, nuns, or just plain Gratefully Single People, each family or individual with a clean, well-lighted room of their own, and vocational tools of their own, but everything else shared—including a spiritual vision. I feel a vision of great simplicity might serve such communites best. Nothing fancy. Let the Calvinists have their "prelapsarianism." A Beguinage's "constitution" could just be some simplified, gospel-spirited statement like, say, the Dalai Lama's remark: "There are many different philosophies, but what is of basic importance is compassion, love for others, concern for others' suffering, and reduction of selfishness."

To live this sweet statement you might start carefully adding a few homeless people, a few sick or dying people, a few orphans to the mix. And your Beguinage is up and running. Picture the kids of this community wandering loose, helping some seventy-year-old Ellen G. White look-alike in

the communal garden for a while, then going swimming or
fishing in the pond while an old aunt or uncle watches—an
aunt or uncle who'd never even glimpse a child or pond if
they lived in a corporate-run retirement home. No individual insurance policies needed, because everyone has agreed
never to sue anyone else, in allegiance to the "reduction of
selfishness" principle. If your house burns, everybody re-
builds it, Amish-style, out of the "concern for others' suffering" principle. And you don't just throw up a HUD house.
You build something beautiful, "to the glory of God." No
need to buy and repair your washer, dryer, freezer, two
cars, or lawn mower in this spiritual community, because
the community shares one industrial-strength washer and
dryer, a small fleet of high-mileage vehicles, and a few sheep
are out mowing the lawn. The moral quandary is: should
we eat one of the lawn mowers now and then? Prob'ly not.
Spiritual community tends to turn even edible animals into
objects of love.

You can see the kind of dream I'm dreaming. It's just
common sense. The Judeo-Suburban Consumer Citadels
so many of us live in grow increasingly nonsensical, even
if you happen to be one of the winners in the system. The
Fossil Fuel Empire grows ever more violent and demonic.
You put busted glass and surveillance cameras on top of
the safety walls and a paid guard at the locked gate of your
Republican Golf Community, and you still get robbed silly
by the insurance scammer, the pool boy, and the guy who
mows the lawn. Or every time you misplace something,
you think you're robbed. It's stupid to live this way if you
have any spiritual aspirations at all! Wouldn't you like to
be able to live your Christian ideals all day long? Wouldn't
you love not to be forced, as we all are daily, to use prod-
ucts produced under toxic or inhumane conditions, often

by children and always by the poor? Isn't it time to dream a better dream?

Let me slide off of this tar baby of a topic by saying that what you call "a communal expression of spiritual wonder" is, to me, not about a church so much as a loving way of living every moment of every day, generation to generation. If we dream big, like the Beguines, they have shown us: it's doable. Just watch out for the world's Pope Gregs!

In closing—and in dreaming further about exactly "What" or "Whom" such a community and its "structure" would be guided by—listen to the visionary architect Christopher Alexander in his masterpiece *The Nature of Order*, volume four, *The Luminous Ground*:

> *Time and again, in one discipline and another, it has been reaffirmed that a pure life can be led only under conditions where one recognizes, and lives, in connection to . . . what some mystics [call] "the ground" or "the void." The fact that this something is nameless, without substance, without form—and yet is also intensely personal—is one of the great mysteries at the source of art. It appears in the writings and teachings of . . . Christian mystics—for example in* The Cloud of Unknowing *and in the writings of William of Wykeham. Essentially similar teachings appear in Zen, in Mahayana Buddhism, in Tibetan Buddhism, in Tantric scriptures, in the spoken word of the Hopi, in the Jewish mystical writings of the Cabala, in the practice of Islam, in the Tao, in the poems and teachings of Sufis like Jalal'a'din Rumi or Shams i-Tabriz, and in the thought of St. Francis of Assisi. The similarity of these teachings has been emphasized many times: "Before heaven and earth, there was something*

nebulous, silent, unchanging and alone, eternal, the Mother of All Things, I do not know its name, I call it Tao."

In every case, the essential point concerns the existence of some realm, or some entity, variously referred to as the Void, the great Self, Paramatma, God, the Friend, and the fact that human life approaches its clear meaning when and only when a person makes contact with this Void. The belief, widely expressed, is that as this connection occurs, the person becomes connected to all things, and at one and the same time more personal, more human, more transparent, and more peaceful. . . .

To make living structure—really to make living structure—it seems almost as though somehow we are charged, for our time, with finding a new form of God, a new way of understanding the deepest origins of our experience, of the matter in the universe so that we too, when lucky, with devotion, might find it possible to reveal this "something" and its blinding light. Yet any new approach to the creation of living structure which is to succeed, cannot be sentimental, cannot be rooted in some old kind of religion. The old kind of religion will not work for most of us and, I think, in its old form, cannot work successfully for us.

It delights me when people I've never met, working in disciplines of which I know little, keep drawing such remarkably similar conclusions. I don't think this could happen unless something wonderful was afoot. I sense that humanity—driven by desperation certainly, but also by love and common sense—is on the verge of getting much more creative in how it lives and believes and shares. We can keep trying to squeeze spirit into the stifling structures the world's Pope Gregs and suburban *Revelation* addicts allow. Or we can sidestep the old religion machines and bring spirited life to new, or resurrected, "living structures." I hope, pray and sense we're within a generation or two of "beginning the Beguines," honoring the Eternal Beloved and Mother of All Things, and finding, deep in our each one's heart, REAL ONE BEING.

"No Great Things . . ."

a talk given to
The Pacific Writers Connection
Honolulu, Hawaii, January 4, 2005

I was given an assignment today. I was asked to speak, specifically, to how writers who revere the natural world—writers who cherish the fragile intricacies of natural systems, species diversity, cultural diversity, spiritual truth—can make a difference in this world in the face of several harsh recent trends.

I'm too ignorant to speak to the writers in this room about Hawaiian or Pacific Rim specifics: for all its problems, Hawaii seems to this outsider like an amazingly progressive place compared to my home in the American West. I can and must speak, though, to a set of problems we lovers of the land all face. It's such an unpleasant topic that a lot of writers have fallen silent in regard to it, as if hoping the unpleasantness will simply go away. I don't see that happening so let me call a spade a spade: the two-headed dragon we writers must engage if we wish to make a difference today are named *neoconservatism* and *Apocalypse-oriented fundamentalism*.

In the good old days of the '90s, when Pat Robertson ran for president, so many people were terrified at the thought of a nuclear-weaponed Armageddonist in the White House that he was handily defeated. The terrain has mysteriously changed. Environmentally, culturally, diplomatically, militarily, and religiously speaking, the equivalent of Pat Robertson *is* president, and we male and female knights who seek a sustainable culture, biological health, compassionate diplomacy, open-hearted spirituality, and an intact world to pass on to our children, have little choice but to don psychic armor and name the neocon/fundamentalist juggernaut for what it is.

For clarity's sake I'd like to divide my talk into little chapterettes. I also promise that, though my talk begins darkly, it won't stay that way. My faith, intuition, and life experience don't allow an unremittingly dark talk. It wouldn't be honest.

1. Three Conservation Debacles

That the dominant force in U.S. politics is called "neoconservatism" is ironic in that its general aims seek to conserve nothing. The Bush administration's economic achievements and stewardship of the earth are the worst in U.S. history. As writers, I feel we're duty-bound to put no weight on editorial generalizations like the two I've just made, but my time is too short to present a comprehensive list of specifics. You surely know that the EPA and other stewardship agencies have been gutted or corrupted by corporate insiders. You probably know that industrial polluters are no longer being fined, and that White House policy on global warming is being determined by the likes of the International Policy Network, which is funded in part by ExxonMobil. But the list is too long and troubling. To cite just three examples of the kinds of destructions we've been witnessing, consider:

1) The Bush administration has *increased* the amount of mercury breathed by Americans for the financial benefit of the coal-fired electricity industry. Diseases both mental and physical, especially in children, and the reckless endangerment of all pregnancies, are "good for bidness" (unless you're the kind of business that would provide our nation with clean, renewable power), so neocons support it.

2) Mountaintop removal coal mining supplies the power plants that force us to inhale, drink, and eat the mercury. This industry—which the Bush administration has facilitated by relaxing safeguards and substituting pseudo-science for environmental science—is literally destroying much of West Virginia, Kentucky, and East Tennessee. Every four days it uses more explosives than the U.S. used in the war in Afghanistan. It crushes entire mountains. It then removes coal, runs poisonous slurry into valley streambeds, places the streams' waters in underground culverts, and buries the valleys those streams had given meandering life to, killing continuously in the process.

3) Pacific salmon, to continue to exist, have nowhere to live but in the ravaged rivers and degraded ocean that industrial humanity bequeaths them. In the 260,000 square miles of the Columbia/Snake River drainage, wild salmon still have a pristine network of inland mountain streams the size of Colorado in which to spawn and grow. Yet they're going extinct, because they're being slaughtered before they can reach these streams, by four unneeded dams on the lower Snake. There are *227 dams over a hundred feet tall* in the Columbia/ Snake system. Just four of them are wiping out the Inland West's last wild salmon. The Bush administration's so-called biological plan for these endangered salmon was to repudiate the most painstaking scientific study of a watershed in history, hijack the English language, and decree, first, that the

words "hatchery salmon" now mean "wild salmon," second, that the word "reservoir" now means "free-flowing river," and third, that the word "dam" now means "natural part of a free-flowing river." All dams, they now say, are "immutable," and "beyond human discretion to reverse." Dams, in other words, are no longer tools meant to serve humanity: they are golden calves before which we are told to bow down so that the administration can negate the Endangered Species Act, render salmon defenders helpless, and send the Northwest's most crucial biological form into oblivion.

2. When Psychosis Sweeps a Nation

The other national malady we face as writers is the politicized, Armageddon-obsessed fundamentalism that tries to dignify such destructions as these by claiming a sense of so-called divine mandate. There are many kinds of fundamentalists. Precious few are devoted earth stewards, but many are big-hearted people. To judge by the conservation voting records of those the Christian Right supports in Congress, however, the majority of fundamentalists see Mother Earth as a trampoline upon which we must stomp, the harder we stomp the more proud of us God will be, for Earth is fleeting, and only here to launch us toward heaven, so why not blow mountains up and dump them as rubble on top of streams, and why not support, from the pulpits of our so-called houses of God, so-called conservative candidates who conserve nothing but corporate profits reaped through our Armageddon-aimed Earth-stomping agenda?

We nonfundamentalist students of the Bible can think of many reasons not to practice such a "faith"—the words, example, and Person of Jesus chief among them. But we seem to find ourselves in a political minority at present.

One duty of a Pacific writer, and every honest soul, is to call destructive madness destructive madness. But apocalyptic fundamentalists and neocons aren't listening to our warnings. If anyone in Kentucky cared about nobility of soul and countless truth-packed warnings, the reluctant philosopher king and queen of that land would be the prophet-farmers Wendell and Tanya Berry, not the mountain-removal industry. But that'll be the day. Corporations now have the rights of medieval kings and queens, and conservatives and fundamentalists have their own pundits and media. When a neocon patriarch proclaims that removing mountaintops, breathing mercury, and worshiping Immutable Dams are more important to America than ecosystem and soul health, right-wing religious loyalists, by gosh, vote in the good ol' boys who'll keep the Golden Calf Dams standing and mountains and mercury falling.

The cofather of psychoanalysis, C. G. Jung, was a great admirer of Jesus. He struggled hard to love his German neighbors back in the early 1930s. But by 1934, Jung had concluded that when psychosis reaches a national scale it has become more powerful than truth, more powerful than reason, and far more powerful than any truth-telling individual.

Jung's observation has hit me in my public-speaking face as I've advocated for ecosystem, watershed, and species health. In speaking for languageless earthlings such as wild salmon, we have little choice but to speak of how human stewardship effects these silent ones—and a great deal of stewardship, in turn, is grounded in policies signed into law by elected officials. Politics then forces ecosystem and species defenders, no matter how apolitical we may be, to learn in a hurry the necessity of discriminating between shitola and shinola. George W. Bush, for example, claimed to an international audience during the presidential debates that he has been "a good steward of the land." Applying the same level of honesty to our gathering today, I am touched to see so many veterans of the War of 1812 seated among us.

The shitola versus shinola problem long ago led me to give up judging politicians by their words. Instead I apply Jesus's dictum: "By their fruits ye shall know them." In honor of this dictum I have, during the hundred or so conservation talks I've given in the past decade, almost always included a list of the conservation deeds and misdeeds of every administration in power. I've done this under Reagan, Bush Senior, Clinton, and Bush Junior. I've tried to do it with no editorial comment and as little emotion as possible, believing that if indeed by their fruits we know them, the public-recorded deeds speak for themselves.

Back in the '90s my lists of conservation shortcomings often angered Clinton's supporters. But they would argue with me, saying stuff like: "If we don't cut *some* of the ancient trees we'll lose the next election and the Republicans will cut *all* the ancient trees." George W's supporters don't argue. Every time I read my list of the fruits by which we know this administration, a bunch of Bush people simply stand up and walk out in a fury. As they see it, my list of the specifics of their president's trashing of Creation is a gratuitous trashing of their president. This reaction is remarkable—and crucial, I feel, in our current attempts to be effective writers. The refusal to hear Bush's actual record implies a certain love of land, there's hope buried here— but also a disconnect. Rather than support a president who would stop unleashing the horrors they're infuriated to hear listed, Bush backers simply want us to stop upsetting them with the dread deeds of their man.

Such people have become closed systems. The biological

devastations caused by their own vote is not something they want to know about. A question for us as writers is: should we go on telling them? I don't claim to own the high ground on this quandary, but I do go on telling. I do so because I don't feel that Jesus was just gratuitously trashing humanity when He warned that the fruits of our deeds shall save or condemn us. I believe He was giving us guidelines for the soul's salvation. This makes it my responsibility, in the attempt to love a neighbor named Bush and his followers, to point out the horrific consequences of his administration's actions—dead three-year-old boys in raped coal valleys, disease and death due to mercury poisoning, and extinct salmon, to reiterate today's three examples.

To their hearts' credit but their imaginations' disgrace, many who are unaware of these devastations insist upon remaining unaware. This, I believe, is the kind of mental impasse C. G. Jung was referring to when he said that national psychosis is more powerful than our power to change it.

Which brings us to the very tough question: what can writers do in the face of such a power?

3. Of Love & Prayer

I don't usually talk about Jesus or Christianity much, but we are living, these days, under the reign of a so-called prayer president who many believe is in office precisely because of his overt references to his prayers and his God. The November postelection AP photo of Jerry Falwell and Karl Rove sharing a stage in triumph is an example of two scary chaps who believe this. Some even say God has given Bush and his administration a "divine mandate."

The reason I so often invoke Jesus in my activist work these days is that there is no better response to this "prayer president" and "mandate" balderdash than the gospels. Politicized fundamentalists are apparently too busy collecting money and votes and consolidating destructive power in Jesus's name to consider His actual words or life. Does no one remember Him advising us to pray "in a closet," shut in, to a "Father who sees in secret" and rewards us only in secret? Does no one remember the order not only to love but to do good to those who hate us? Does no one recall that it is the meek and the weak, the pure in heart and poor in spirit, the peacemakers and the merciful who are blessed by this astonishing man? Does no one any longer preach that the lilies of the field are to be considered for their blithe beauty, that the fowls of the air are to be imitated for their nonhoarding trust in each day that dawns, that the *"fish shall be according to their kinds . . . exceeding many,"* and that the waters of life are to be loved and listened to, not covered in mining rubble in the name of the neocon prophet, Profit?

I don't like wearing my spiritual heart on my sleeve, but in response to the coronation of a so-called prayer president whose dark fruits horrify every earth lover I know, it feels relevant to mention that millions of "we the horrified" *also* pray, day and night. We just happen to do it in our closets as the gospels recommend. Though I refuse to pray on even this benign Honolulu "street corner," I will say a few words about my relationship with prayer.

The only unfailing guide I've ever found through the innumerable blind alleys of my life as a writer, man, husband, father, citizen, steward, or believer, is the love burning in my heart. For me, prayer is about one thing: *making contact with that love.* Though it burns in there like a candle flame, hot, bright, beautiful, love's flame is fragile: so fragile, I feel, that the wrong kind of prayer can snuff it out; so fragile, I sense, that it absolutely *needs* the stillness of "the closet" Jesus recommends in order to burn brightly. So to the prayer president and every other proponent of mass piety and public prayer, I say *Matthew 6:6 forever*. If prayer now means we talk *to* the Flame of Love, on TVs and street corners, telling It what *we* desire rather than seeking Its guidance, then to hell with prayer. If prayer means proclaiming to the world that America is the source of this Eternal Flame and that U.S. fundamentalists are the Chief Spokespersons for God on earth, to hell with prayer. If the wordless yearning or brokenhearted sigh of the Muslim and Jew and Buddhist nun and wordless child and brujo and kahuna at prayer is not equally pleasing to the One True Listener, to hell with prayer. If prayer is now a means of coldcocking the powers of reason that Jefferson swore democracy would die without, if prayer is a means of wooing votes, if prayer has ceased to marvel at an unspeakably sublime Mystery and is now a public gloat about a "mandate" gained through media onslaught, half-truths, military might, cathode-ray distortions of reality, and outright lies, to hell with prayer.

Keeping one's love burning, and living in accord with that burning: this, to me, is prayer. And love, as the gospels describe it, is not the glorification of self, but the renunciation of it for the sake of the beloved, whether that beloved be God, the words of Jesus, a woman, a child, a doomed salmon run, or an annihilated mountain in East Tennessee.

When prayer comes to mean asking for ends that please *me* first and foremost, God help me *stop* praying: help me love something or someone instead.

4. Peacemakers & Lizard People

I've been preserving my sanity for years now with two sentences of Mother Teresa's, and recommend that all writers of faith might try the same. The first great Mama T sentence (which helped me survive the November '04 election) goes like this: "*God doesn't ask us to win. He asks us to try.*"

Like every nature lover I know, I tried my best to speak and write words that would end the Bush administration's rule last fall. I then tried to detach from that effort, prayerfully and completely. I worked all day on election day—on a comedy novel about reincarnation and karma. Comedy is as endangered as wild salmon in this dark time. I felt so determined not to lose an hour to the squalid political theatre that has swallowed so many peoples' attentiveness and sense of hope that I read no paper, listened to no radio, and put in a productive day.

At about 4 P.M. though, I somehow knew in my bones that Bush was going to win. This intuition produced a lump of grief so cold and hard that I could not write another sentence. I stared out the window for a while. It's beautiful out my window. The lump in my throat was so cold and hard I may as well have been blind.

Needing church—which I have to admit I define as "two or *less* gathered in His Name"—I went looking for my neighbor, John. John's a New Mexican, a fine fisherman, a scholar-carpenter, a mystic fan of our Lady of Guadalupe, a conservation activist, and a thoughtful friend. I found him working on cabinets for a bathroom remodel, his radio concertedly *off*, as determined as I'd been not to lose a day's work to despair. But there is also a mental state, called denial, that can get you into trouble if you don't face what's in your face. An exceptionally wise nurse I know—Ivy Push, from the Queen's Medical Center in Honolulu—has this to say of grief's denial: "The only cure for grief is a pill, called *Grief*. And if you don't take your medicine, you won't get well."

As I looked at John, I realized the thing stuck in my

throat was this very pill, and it felt the size of a major league baseball. When John looked back at me, I could tell by his eyes that he was choking on the same pill. "Do you feel what I feel?" I asked.

"Shit," big strong John murmured, shaking his head the way that helps you not cry.

Time to swallow. But what could wash this pill down?

I said, "I think it might be healthful for both of us if, on every day on which somebody named Bush is elected to public office for the rest of our lives, we knock off a little early and have ourselves a stiff dram of scotch."

John and I dubbed this agreement the Lolo Accord, signed it immediately into law, and our stiff drams proved healthful indeed. I've got this highland druidic thing lurking in my blood: as soon as single malt touches my lips, all I can think or talk about are the archangels, hidden masters, ragged sheikhs, and mystic poets who I believe really run things here on earth. John's got the New Mexican version of the same deal. One sip of the fire in water and he began telling of a friend of his, new to visionary experience, who'd recently sought counsel from a Brazilian shaman. The friend had been traumatized, during a lengthy initiation rite, when he had a vision of a bunch of fearsome, remorseless Reptile Beings. The Reptile Men surrounded John's terrified friend, informed him that they controlled the entire world, and prophesied that they were going to devour the whole thing.

In response to this revelation, the old shaman waved his hand dismissively and chuckled, "Those Lizard People! They think they run everything."

I thought: *Operation Infinite Justice*. I thought: *Shock and Awe*. I thought: *Those Lizard People!* But God just asks us to try. Not to win. So I said nothing aloud.

And that's as close as John and I came to discussing the election. The next morning we both went back to work, not winning, but still trying—and enjoying the effort.

If I were to add anything to Mother Teresa's quote I'd remind us that vast numbers of compassionate and remarkable people, unbeknownst to us, are trying right alongside us. Wendell Berry emphasized this unconsolidated, global unanimity of purpose in a recent talk in Missoula, and expressed the hope that these droves of great hearts would organize. Those of us who travel and address groups like Pacific Writers get to see and enjoy this hidden unanimity frequently. Wendell's mere appearance caused a huge crowd of such people to appear in Missoula: a crowd whose faces shone with kindness and intelligence and looked like it supported organic-sustainable-small-scale-socially-responsible EVERYTHING. Yet I'd never seen most of them before. They'd simply come out of the Montana woodwork in response to the magic word "Wendell." Based on extensive travels and talks of my own, I tell you: such people are *everywhere*.

Too many of us forget, in part because corporate-controlled mass media try to make us forget, that an event such as the worldwide protest against the Iraq War in February 2003 was unprecedented in history and bespeaks a marvelous global yearning for change. On a single day, hundreds of millions of people marched in more than six hundred cities worldwide, nonviolently begging the U.S. not to go to preemptive war and create an unholy quagmire. The website of photos of several hundred of these marches moved me to tears—but got no media play in America. Some believe a billion people marched that day: one of every six earthlings. The smallest estimates say it was more than six hundred million: two and a half times as many people as live in the States.

The "prayer president's" remark about the greatest peace march in world history: *"I don't listen to focus groups."*

Jesus's remark about it: *"Blessed are the peacemakers."*

5. "No Great Things . . ."

The second Mother Teresa quote that's been saving my sanity: *"We can do no great things—only small things, with great love."*

This woman, we tend to forget, helped homeless Calcuttans one sick or dying person at a time. This means, in a sense, that she *ignored* the hundreds of thousands who were also in dire need in the world in her time. She did not take this approach because she did not wish to help *all* the sick and dying. She'd simply realized: *we can do no great things.* And, sweet irony, the skein of small things she so lovingly did won her a following that continues to do small, beautiful things for the helpless and hopeless to this day.

The day I rediscovered Mother Teresa's words, the so-called war on terror had just cranked up, and the Rumsfeld/ Cheney Crew were dignifying the call to violence with rhetoric so over-the-top it abrogated divine authority, "Operation Infinite Justice" being the most spectacularly sad example. What a grounded, utterly human antidote, the words, *"We can do no great things—only small things, with great love."* Mama T's formula, at the dire time I rediscovered it, released so much pressure that I could breathe and relax my neck and shoulders and smile again. Instead of waking each morning and defining myself as an impotent war protester in an America run by oil-worshipping thugs, I started waking up and thinking: "Okay. What small thing can I do today with love?"

What a relief! Mother's advice gave me permission to

do stuff like play with my kids and go fishing again. This may seem digressive, but I actually live Mother T's advice when I fish. No joke. On big Montana trout rivers like the Missouri, lower Clark Fork, Blackfoot, you often see fly fishers trying to "do great things" by "fishing heroically," making great long casts out into the giant flow as if they're thinking *OPERATION INFINITE TROUT!* But "we can do no great things." So those of us who like to actually catch trout scarcely glance at the vast flow. Instead we parse the river, slicing off a tiny slice known as a "feeding lane" where, if a trout is holding and bugs are hatching, you target a single trout, repeatedly rising. In huge Western rivers, three or four hundred feet wide in places, I'm talking about a ribbon six inches in width. Yet this ribbon, believe me, is where all the rising trout get hooked.

A fly-fisherly writing strategy you Pacific Writers could import from Montana in order to keep "making a difference": *every morning, look for "ribbons." One person in need. One deft paragraph to complete. One smile for a stranger. One small thing you sense could be done with full-on attentiveness and love. And after you finish it, look for another one. Ad infinitum.*

I don't know about you all, but I'm hopelessly flawed. This is another reason I love Mother Teresa's advice. When small things are done with love it's not a flawed you or me who does them: it's love. I have no faith in any kind of political party, left, right, or centrist. I have boundless faith in love. In keeping with this faith, the only spiritually responsible way I know to be a citizen, artist, or activist in these strange times is by giving little or no thought to "great things" such as saving the planet, achieving world peace, or stopping neocon greed. Great things tend to be undoable things. Whereas small things, lovingly done, are always within our reach.

Politics, these days, are about such great things that they somehow end up being about nothing. Politics, increasingly, are about winning elections at all cost via the violent manipulation of human opinion. But no climate of mere opinion is earnest enough, or embodied enough, to answer our biological and spiritual predicament from moment to moment in daily life.

The natural systems and elemental forces that give us bodies and lives are rife with simple integrity and sincerity of purpose. The maneuverings of political factions blind us to this integrity, or make us think we can fool it. But you can't use a glib skit and laugh track to joke a polar ice cap into not melting. You can't hire a PR firm to fast-talk radioactivity out of nuclear wastes. You can't hire Rove, Rush, or Coulter to sneer the carcinogens out of the Columbia or alkalinity out of the Colorado. Watch a mated pair of Bullock's orioles build their incredible hanging nest not in the thirty seconds it takes to brainwash a voter but for the days and days it needs to be properly built. Watch a female salmon turn her body into a shovel and beat it into the stone bed of a high mountain stream, smashing aside rock not for the quarter hour it takes a "commentator" to make a string of partisan wisecracks, but for the three or four arduous nights and days it takes to build a redd that can house and protect living progeny.

There is no disingenuousness in the life-giving operations of nature, nothing snide, nothing needlessly clever— for which reason there can be no disingenuousness in our stewardship of these life-giving operations. In response to nature's sincerity I'm trying to live, and to celebrate in many kinds of words and deeds, a dead-earnest, though far from humorless, Mother Teresian politics of no politics, no longer fretting the huge things I can't change, focusing instead on one small thing after another, driven, each time, by the greatest possible love. And dark as the times may be, this politics of no politics has been bringing me a steady sense of purpose, and surprisingly frequent feelings of outright joy.

I wish I had time to tell ten stories about the power of small things I've recently seen done with love, and the inordinate amount of energy and courage people, including me, have gleaned from partaking in these small things. I have time for two such stories.

Here's the first.

6. A Small School for Liam

On June 10, 1999, a seam burst in the pipeline that links Seattle/Tacoma to the Alaskan oil fields, and some 300,000 gallons of gasoline spilled into Whatcom Creek, the beautiful little salmon and steelhead stream that bisects Bellingham, Washington's downtown. The gas was then accidentally ignited by two ten-year-olds playing with a bottle rocket—setting off an explosion in downtown Bellingham that looked nuclear. Both ten-year-olds died, and not quickly. Their courage was heartbreaking. One of the paramedics who tended them quit the profession because of what he saw.

The third victim of the explosion, Liam Wood, was eighteen years old. He'd just finished high school, had an afternoon off from his job at a local fly shop, and had elected to spend it as I would have at his age: fly-fishing Whatcom Creek. So much gas came downstream that Liam was overcome by the fumes, fell facedown in the creek, and drowned before the explosion and fire. On his bedroom floor he left his high school diploma, a note to his mom saying he'd be home for dinner, and a copy of my first novel, *The River Why*, which he'd read something like eight times.

Liam's fate left me heartsick for many reasons. I have twice stood in urban creeks at the moment effluent was causing their fish to turn belly up. Both times I headed upstream to try to find the source of the damage. Liam's friends believe he did the same, instead of running, and that his allegiance to Whatcom Creek cost him his life. My activist anger also kicked in when I learned that Liam's mom, Marlene Robinson, and the two ten-year-olds' parents, testified to various agencies about the danger of gas pipelines, but were greeted largely with arrogance and indifference. When Marlene talked to a congressional committee in Washington, D.C., for instance, the congresspersons were moved and alarmed by her story—and what a hellish tale to have to dredge up in front of strangers. Seeing the disturbance her testimony caused among "their" congresspeople, though, oil industry lobbyists came scurrying in to remind the legislators of their obligations before Marlene had even left the room.

For a while I just fumed at this. Then it occurred to me to seek some small thing that might ease the fuming. This turned me immediately toward the things that Liam Wood had loved. He was a beloved young man, so after he died a lot was written about him. He'd been a legendary fly fisher, was a gifted aspiring writer, and was a budding conservationist who'd worked on salmon restoration in, among other places, the very stream in which he died.

Asking myself what small thing might carry on the loves of such an astute young fly fisher, I was drawn to a remark made by Liam's mom in an interview I'd read: Marlene told her interviewer that the thing helping her most with her grief was doing restoration work down on poor, burned-up little Whatcom Creek. The article included a photo of her there, pushing a wheelbarrow through the blackened spars of trees.

Fly-fishing son. Restoration-loving mother. Small things. Love. I had a little dream regarding Liam, and wrote it down. When I gave a reading in Bellingham in 2001, I shared this dream with his mom and stepdad, Bruce. They then shared it with others, and a little avalanche of hope and goodwill got rolling.

The result: we have started a little river lover's school— The Liam Wood Flyfishing and River Guardian School. In July 2004, we graduated our first seventeen students. A small thing, to be sure, but there's not one thing about it that those who knew Liam don't think he would have loved. People as far away as Iowa and Wyoming ended up wanting in. All our grads said they planned to get involved in stream restoration work afterward. Our class evaluations said stuff like, "Not only the best class I've ever taken, but the best class I EVER expect to take."

For the bargain price of $400—with scholarships for those in need—our prototype class gave students instruction in fly-fishing, fly-tying, fly-casting; they studied literature, films and movies, both documentary and drama, on rivers and rehab and fishing; they took stream stewardship field trips and enjoyed a skein of larks on what they dubbed "Fly-fishing Fridays"; they did lab work on water quality, studied onstream demonstrations of hydrology, ecological processes, environmental history, salmon recovery projects; they had class visits from fishing guides, rodbuilders, master-tyers, stream rehab experts, fisheries biologists; and the climactic "small thing" was a fly-fishing excursion to the headwaters of the Whatchamacallit River in British Columbia (the first overnight fly-fishing trip for most students), where they were joined by Ian Muirhead, a legendary guide and fly-fishing ethics teacher from Roderick

Haig-Brown House in Canada, and by a semilegendary literary river coot from Montana.

Another small but fine thing: among our students was my new friend, Liam's stepdad, Bruce, a fine man who did not formerly fly-fish, but found he missed Liam less when he began to share, rather than just mourn, his lad's love of the waters.

Over the next few years we hope to open Liam Wood "branch offices" in Eugene or Corvallis, Oregon, where Liam first learned to fish. People are throwing money and fly gear and support at us. Not a few of these benefactors are Bush supporters. Go figure! It's a small thing we've done, and we can't bring back this great human being or erase the senselessness from his demise. But some of our students have had something tangible to do with the fact that Liam's beloved Whatcom Creek has made a comeback after being burned lifeless—salmon and trout are again spawning in it in droves. And at our party at the end of the first run of classes—when a boy's loves filled a dining room with laughter and left his hometown a small legacy—the smiles that passed over Marlene's and Bruce's faces, though still understandably sad, were surely a far cry from their expressions the day Marlene testified in D.C.

7. Convergence of Ambrose & Blix

My final tale of a Mother Teresian small thing:

Hans Blix is an honorable, eloquent European disliked by some Americans on the political right for having told the world, truthfully it turned out, that there was no evidence of weapons of mass destruction in Iraq before America invaded. Stephen Ambrose was an American historian renowned for his scholarship, his patriotism, his admiration of World War II vets, and his voluminous knowledge of the courage and sacrifices that have given our nation its unique character. When the Trade Towers fell in 2001, Ambrose publicly raged that Afghanistan should be "bombed back to the Stone Age." Not a sentiment with which Blix would see eye to eye. That's precisely what makes this a good story.

At the end of Blix's duties as chief U.N. weapons inspector, he told Charlie Rose that wars did not frighten him as much as they used to, because international peacekeeping looks likely to work well enough that no war will again achieve the world scale of those of the last century. "This may surprise you," Blix said, "but what I believe threatens us most, now, is what our industry and our increasing numbers have done to the life support systems of this earth." Environmental crises, Blix predicted, will be the headlines of the coming century.

As he was dying of lung cancer at the same time, the patriot historian Ambrose came to the very same conclusion, but framed the crisis in more hopeful terms. "The 21st century," he declared, "will be the century of restoration."

As a longtime soldier in the service of rivers, I'm thrilled to report that Ambrose walked his restoration talk: one of his last acts was to pledge $250,000 dollars to a watershed watchdog group, the Clark Fork Coalition, in my hometown, Missoula. That's a huge amount of money for the Coalition. The historian made his pledge because he knew they were attempting something truly historic: standing up to a monolithic Montana legend, Anaconda Copper, now owned by the even more monolithic ARCO/British Petroleum. One of the things ARCO/BP inherited, when they purchased Anaconda Copper, was six million square yards of toxic mining wastes on the bottom of the reservoir behind Milltown Dam. This dam stands at the confluence of the Clark Fork and Big Blackfoot Rivers—the river in *A River Runs Through It.* The bulk of the wastes arrived during the flood of 1908, which washed decades worth of Anaconda Copper pollution into the reservoir. One poison now leaching into groundwater there is arsenic: it had been drunk for years by the families of Milltown before it was discovered. The Milltown dam is a century old. It is full of cracks, nearly bursts during floods, stops migration of threatened bull trout, and generates so little hydroelectricity that it operates at a loss.

Before it was purchased by British Petroleum, ARCO answered the outcry of our water guardians with some of the most specious pro-dam arguments I've yet heard (and I thought I'd heard them all, over on the lower Snake River). One argument was that the removal of any dam, even a potential catastrophe dam like the Milltown, would encourage those who will remove *all* dams everywhere. As if any such lunatics could succeed if they even existed. Another remarkable ARCO move was the creation of a fake "grass roots" organization that claimed to be interested in saving "historic structures," such as this dam, simply because they were "historic." This was precisely why Stephen Ambrose was such a powerful voice in our fight. The great historian knew exactly how "historic" Milltown dam was: that's why he pledged a quarter million to tear the goddamned thing down.

Lacking that kind of cash, I could do no great things to help. But I could still attempt a few "small things with great love." On the day I composed a bumper sticker for ARCO's fake grassroots group, my love felt a lot like caustic fury, but God help me, I was trying. My bumper sticker read:

PRESERVE TOXIC WASTES!
DON'T MAKE ARCO CLEAN UP ITS MESS!
LET KIDS DRINK ARSENIC!
SAVE HISTORIC MILLTOWN DAM!

ARCO's faux "grass rooters" did not deploy my bumper sticker.

British Petroleum was the first oil giant to go on record saying that the era of fossil fuels is at its end. BP has also invested in serious potential alternatives. So when BP bought ARCO, we begin to feel some hope. Before the Clark Fork Coalition could ascertain BP's position on removing the dam and toxic sludge, though, who should enter the fray but the Bush administration? And guess whose side they took?

Claiming that their dictatorial decree would "stimulate the economy," the Bush braintrust stonewalled new scientific research on arsenic poisoning, blocked new legislation in keeping with this research, and left the amount of arsenic allowed in the drinking water of human beings at cumulatively lethal levels. Isn't freedom great? Thanks to the democratic vote of NOBODY, King George the Bush's minions kept the Milltown Dam operating inside "the law" so that the children of Bonner and Milltown were "free," as young Americans in times of terror, to drink poison!

Ah, but money is money, and a dying patriot named Ambrose pledged a quarter million units of the stuff to one of the feistiest little watchdog groups on earth. Though Ambrose only lived long enough to pay a fifth of his pledge, the mere legend of it caused the river's abusers to fear not just the usual conservationist wrath, but the wrath of bona fide right-wing conservatives and good ol' boys. The dam defenders began to waver even despite the mighty Bush.

The Clark Fork Coalition, meanwhile, used Ambrose's and other donations to educate the public. Our opposition to dam and sludge grew more public, more artful, and more organized. The Coalition marshaled the press and negated ARCO propaganda point by point for *years*. They put together a lovely anthology of Clark Fork writings, to which the painter, Russell Chatham, donated beautiful original lithographs and a score or so of us writers donated stories and essays. They organized a huge anti-dam flotilla down the river, in which thousands of people participated. The comic highlight of that float, for my then-nine- and eleven-year-old daughters, were the fake grassroots protest placards that ARCO posted along the river. Their still-quoted favorite read "SAVE THE DAM, KILL THE HIPPIE!" How bipartisanly ironic that the "hippie" most responsible for our massive show of clean-water-love was the short-haired, flag-saluting, vet-embracing, patriot historian, Stephen Ambrose.

The first big float ended in a free public concert where the beer kegs, which were not free, raised more anti-arsenic money. (The float was so much fun it's now an annual event.) The Coalition, meanwhile, continued to pressure the corporate heads till, about a year after Ambrose died, the key players met face to face and realized that, though we can do no great things, even mega-corporations can do an occasional small, unprofitable thing out of love—even if it's just love of good publicity.

Thus has one golden calf of a dam proven less than "immutable." Three small but lovingly done acts of restoration Ambrose's Century of Restoration are sure enough going to see are the removal of "historic" Milltown Dam, the removal and containment of millions of square yards of historic toxic sludge, and the elimination of all that Bush-approved arsenic kids could otherwise be drinking.

Though the dam will stand another year, the release of restoration money already has a hundred-mile river returning to life. Heavy metals are being contained, toxic trouts' offspring will soon be edible, and the valley's waterfowl, wildlife, ranches, and small businesses are showing vital and interwoven signs of flourishing.

I wish I had time for a dozen more Small-Things-with-Great-Love Stories. Mama T's advice is not, I don't feel, just a sanity saver. I believe it could save more than a few souls from succumbing to the darkness of our times.

Why do I so strongly believe this? Because one such soul is mine.

Agony & Hilarity

One night a few Novembers ago I traveled into Missoula along with my tin whistles, dreadfully electrified mountain dulcimer, a pile of poetry and yarns, and my fearless friend the pianist Philip Aaberg, where a church loaned us itself and its piano, and I offered my services as the cacophonous half of an Aaberg & Duncan fundraising concert/reading for the famed Montana fly fisher, Gary LaFontaine, shortly before Gary died of Lou Gehrig's disease.

I was just back from New York. Phil was just back from touring with the guitarist Roy Rogers. (No, not *that* Roy Rogers!) Since we had no time to rehearse, we billed our performance as a public rehearsal. A good crowd came anyway. Phil and I then played and read a combination of stories, poems, and music that ranged from the forthrightly ridiculous to the darned-near sublime, in attempted illustration of the great Norman Maclean axiom: "Agony and hilarity are both necessary for salvation."

Gary came to our performance—in a wheelchair, diapers, and pretty rough shape. But as often happens at such occasions, it was Phil and I who received the benefit of our supposed philanthropy. When we were done with our stuff and nonsense and most of the crowd had gone home, Gary somehow found the energy to tell us how much he'd enjoyed himself, then spoke of what he called "the gift" of knowing that his end was nigh—gift of receiving the countless expressions of love and affection this hard fact had inspired. He then began to rhapsodize—even as he ran out of breath and his head began dropping to his chest—about his endless love for rivers, wilderness, high lakes, fish, fisherfolk, fishing implements, fishing literature, fishing dogs (especially his own Chester), fishing maniacs, and fly-fishing, fly-fishing, fly-fishing.

One of the beliefs of this deeply eccentric fishing maestro was in what he called "perfect moments." Gary held that this world, as altered by industrial man, has gone insane, but that by using a combination of love, fly gear, and (Gary's trademark twist) "the empirical method," we could cut the insanity out by carefully designing potential "perfect moments." The way many such moments then blew up in our faces, Gary felt, made the moments that worked out all the more perfect. He held, further, that a skilled and determined seeker of such moments could convert their life into a stream of dark and light perfections that flowed through them even amid deep adversity—even, say, in a wheelchair and diapers.

Hearing this exquisite nonsense from a guy who'd just spent years nursing a wife with cancer, only to lose her and immediately be diagnosed with Gehrig's—hearing a dying man, with his daughter standing in front of him, speak with penultimate gratitude and even an anguished joy about his ending life—made my year and Philip's too. So I want to reproduce from our performance the story Gary seemed to like best.

I began this particular story by quoting Norman Maclean's statement about agony and hilarity. I then explained to our audience that most of the public speaking I do is to green or watery activist groups interested in saving things. One reason I like talking to such groups, I said, is practical: I love rivers, wilderness, and wild critters, including those wild animals, my kids, and these groups fight for the life and health of my loves—so we're saprophytic, or incestuous, or whatever the scientific term may be.

But another reason I like addressing such groups, I confessed, might be more to Norman Maclean's liking. Inevitably I find, lurking among activist groups, some of the most highly principled, one-pointed, *humorless* people on earth. For reasons I can't rationally explain—personal behavior patterns as innate as those of ravens, I suppose—I enjoy trying to reach across the division between humorous and solemn souls by telling stories that show both agony *and* hilarity to be necessary for the salvation of things.

Last fall I'd given such a talk to a river protection organization—a talk heavy on the joys, heartbreaks, and insights gleaned through a lifetime of fly-fishing. I was doing a Q & A afterward, when a grave-looking young woman asked something I've been asked many times before. She said, "How can you sound so spiritual about catch and release fly-fishing, when all it really amounts to is senseless torture of the fish?"

When people make this accusation it always freezes me for a moment, not because I have no reply, but because I have so many that they ram together in my head like a ten-car collision.

My initial response to the animal rights person was earnest. I first admitted that, yes, catch and release fly-fishing does torment trout. What's more: actually clobbering, killing, gutting, and eating a trout, which I still occasionally like to do, actually clobbers, kills, and guts the trout. Yet, strange to say, we torturer-predators love our prey—and for that reason husband it. If it weren't for duck hunters we would have few surviving wetlands in the lower forty-eight, and few if any surviving wild ducks. The same holds true for fly fishers: we have turned our fondness for inflicting torment upon fish into advocacy groups that have in thousands of cases created better conditions for trout, rivers, and the wildlife dependent on both.

For this reason, I explained, I think of the trout's torment as their way of participating in democracy. There are Yellowstone cutthroat living in the lower end of Slough Creek which biologists estimate are caught and released as many as 300 times in a seven-year life span. That's a lot of democracy! On the other hand, it's 300 direct, one-on-one battles between a land being and a river being, ending with 300 stunned urbanites kneeling, one at a time, in crystalline waters, with their heart pounding and hands shaking, wondering whether a more beautiful creature has ever existed in a more beautiful place—and feeling beautiful themselves for a moment, for having captured and communed with such a being. The result, I told the woman who called me a torturer, is that deceptively simple word: love. Which leads to a more complicated word: allegiance—to healthy wild waters, gorgeous wild fish, wild lands. The trout being caught by fly fishers silently lobby us, if you will, by giving us amazing experiences that translate into river and fish advocacy on the part of groups like Washington Trout, Trout Unlimited, Save Our Wild Salmon, the Outdoor Conservation Alliance, trout dweeb Yvon Chouinard's great One Percent for the Earth corporate tithing program, and on and on and on.

I've laid this argument out a lot of times. The fiercest critics of fly-fishing refuse to buy it. The young woman at this lecture proved such a critic: animal rights activists such as herself, she informed us, do not believe that a trout should have to lobby some damned human in order to exist in peace. A trout, she said, has the same basic right to exist as we in the lecture hall did, and if we truly loved them we would defend them without fishing for them. Therefore, she said, despite my pseudo-ethical gymnastics, I was still just an inexcusable trout torturer.

The woman's tenacity and eloquence impressed me. They also pissed me off. This in turn caused me to breathe deeply, as I have trained myself to do through the years, set aside my hot little head, and sink into the heart—an organ that I find, if you have the faith and know how to surrender to it, unfolds and unfolds in a most wonderful and unscientific manner, till it becomes the vastest and most pristine wilderness in existence.

I did this. I unfolded my heart. And inside its wild vastness my anger gave way to sudden affection for the feisty young activist. My joy in the heart's vastness, moreover, made me feel there might be a way to help her grow aware of her own interior vastness, and so perhaps become a bit less doctrinaire. A way to do this, I thought, might be to improvise a story that combined the agony of trout with a little hilarity and so, hopefully, raised my antagonist and me above the level of our impasse. To lead into my story I asked the activist herself a question.

I said: "Uh, what about insect rights?"

By way of answer she went, "Hrunnnh?" and made a funny, confused face. I felt I was definitely on the right track.

"Fly fishers are called fly fishers," I continued, "because our flies imitate insects. We are insect aficionados, insect admirers—or, to use a term you might prefer, *insect rights activists.*"

Her lips vanished. Her eyes narrowed. Her brow furrowed. Her nose crinkled. And as the ski dudes say, It Was All Good.

"As an insect rights activist," I continued, "I'd like to ask, if you don't mind: what about the aquatic bug's perspective? Is it only mega fauna that deserve our sympathy? Does your concern for the rights of others cut off at some point when the life-forms get small? What did Laotse mean when he said, *'As good sight means seeing what is very small, so strength means holding on to what is weak.'* We fly-fishers think he might mean that mayflies, stone flies, caddis flies, and such are small, weak, wondrous creatures endowed with the same right to exist as trout, you, and me—and *have you seen what trout do to them?"*

The animal rights woman looked as if I'd lost the point of her protest entirely.

"Think about it," I urged her. "Aquatic bugs are living miracles. Every caddis fly on earth, for instance, knows, without even having to attend school, how to build itself a mobile home out of bits of river gravel, crawl inside the thing, and drive it around the bottom of the river like it's Arizona down there and he or she's from Wisconsin and it's winter so hey, let's pack up the Winnebago an' go campin'.

"And a hatch of caddises—a mass conversion of nymphs into flies—is an eruption of miracles. A huge caddis hatch is the insect world's rendition of the Baptist notion of 'Rapture': millions of those cute little RVs abandoned, down on the river bottom, as up swim the previous owners to the surface and away they fly into the heavens, an inspiration to fundamentalists everywhere. And to console those of us who aren't fundamentalists, all those abandoned casings on the bottom remind us of that great bumper sticker:

IN CASE OF RAPTURE,
CAN I HAVE YOUR CAR?

The animal rights woman now looked as if she feared I'd gone mad. But the miracles of nature *are* a kind of madness. So I invited her to consider another mad miracle: mayflies.

"Mayflies," I said, "begin life as fertilized eggs the size of a speck of fine ground black pepper. That such a speck can figure out, all on its own, how to grow six gracefully curved and articulated legs, and not one but three delicate tails, and not two but four gossamer wings, and a suit of armor, the exoskeleton, which it sheds not once but as many as a hundred times as it grows: more miracles! The variety of mayflies, the extreme range of shapes, colors, sizes, the harmlessness of them, astound me. Not one of these sun-fathered river-mothered insects bite, sting, whine, or harass. Adult mayflies don't even have mouths to harass with. After spending a year underwater as a nymph, there comes an evening when they are moved to swim, for the first time ever, to the river's surface, shed the armor they've spent their life in, slide their tender nude bodies out into the open, seal their jaws shut, and commence a fast that will last the rest of their lives. They then open transluscent wings they hadn't even known they owned, dry them even as they navigate, like rafters, downriver, then flutter up into a ray of sunlight, where they gather with other mayflies, all of them hovering like angels—in order to mate like rabbits!

"Think about leaving everything you know behind and sealing your lips shut forever," I said to the now hopelessly confused animal rights woman, "to rise, naked and fasting, up into the sky, meet with other silent ones like yourself, copulate with them, and so preserve your kind and kingdom forever! Talk about sexy spiritual beings! If our human heaven is even half that interesting, I can't wait to die!

"So before one declares fly-fishing unjust," I advised her, "we might spend a few hours during an intense hatch (a.k.a. Rapture) of mayflies, watching those vicious opportunists, the trout, slashing, maiming and devouring in a mayfly-rights-violating frenzy! Before we declare fly-fishing unjust, we might study those monsters, the *salmonids*, careening along the surface like nuclear subs amongst a hatch of wind-surfers, crunching and gulping victims before they can even open sails. And who in all this sorrowful world is willing to invest the time and extreme care needed to defend the angelic mayflies as Laotse advised? What creature of any description, infernal, terrestrial, or angelic, possesses the skill, patience, and half-insane eccentricity to actually slow the remorseless slaughter—

"—'til a wily fly-fisher sneaks up to river's edge, makes a long, light cast out into the orgy, and an artful scrap of Divine Justice alights on the surface in the form of, say, a size #16 Gray Drake, then floats its way down toward the gorging trout?

"*Touché!* the mouthless, hapless mayflies think each time they see a trout, hooked by a fly-fisher, leaping in sudden panic. And imagine—this is the *really* great part!—the Twilight Zone tales the trout tell their fellow trout *after* they've been caught and released. It's an insect or animal rights dream come true!

"Picture a fresh-caught and released eighteen-inch rain-bow with a mouth tough as a steel nutcracker, unharmed but for an acupuncture wound in its steel, but huffing from exhaustion, and psychically thunderstruck, as it swims back to its run after losing a battle with a fly fisher.

"Seeing it skulking in the weeds, afraid to move, the other trout (mouths stuffed full of innocent mayflies) ask: 'Hey Fiff! Wud's wid choo? Duh bugs're rummy! Crum on up'n' munch!'

" 'I *was!*' gasps the enlightened trout. 'I was inhalin' may-flies like popcorn, just like you guys, when all of a sudden this little drake, no bigger'n one o' my teeth, stings me in the jaw. *Jeezle Peet!* I think, an' shoot out water to spit it. Bug won't spit! Just keeps stingin'! I shake my whole body to twist it loose. This only infuriates it! It starts draggin' me by the jaw all over the damn river! I'm a two-pound trout! The bug weighs what, a thousandth of an ounce? It's embarras-sin'! I try to kill it by chompin' it, try jumpin' to get rid of it, swim fast as lightnin' to outrun it. Nothin' works! I go one way, it drags me the other! I dive for bottom, it hauls me up top! It's tiny, it's ridiculous, it's straight from hell! *That lil' bug beat the livin' shit outta me!* Finally I'm wasted, I'm thrashin' on my side. It won, I think. I'm a broken fish. But it's tired too, surely. It'll let me go now.

" 'The demon bug drags my ass right up on dry land! It's strong as a freakin' moose! Beatin' me senseless only made it hungry! It's gonna eat me, I realize, tiny as it is. An' I'm frickin' freakin'—'cause it's *fair! Goodbye river, goodbye moon and sun, I've had it,* I'm thinkin'...

" 'Except—you guys won't believe this part! Right where the mayfly dragged me out of the water, this nice fly-fisher happens to be standin'! An' no sooner does he see me than he rescues me! Pulls the demon drake outta my lip, cradles me like his own baby there in the shallows, releases me into the current just as nice as you please.' "

"The other trout are gawking. 'You have got to be kid-din'!' they say.

"'Kiddin'?' says the caught and released trout.'Man, I'm prayin'! From this day forward, my prayer is: *Thank God for fly fishers!*'"

The night I first concocted this story another natural miracle happened: a young animal rights activist and an incurable fly fisher made friends. Her face was unreadable when she first approached. She then extended her hand, and shook mine, simultaneously shaking her head like the big trout in the story had done. "I felt caught and released," she graciously confessed.

And even better was the sight Phil Aaberg and I saw when I later recounted this diplomatic breakthrough: a guy in our audience—an apostle of perfect moments and fly fisher of the most unapologetically dweeby sort—all bent over in the wilderness of his diapers and wheelchair in the last couple weeks of life, laughing like there is no tomorrow.

Norman Maclean was so smart: agony and hilarity both.

De-bore-HA!

*my first & last work of christic fiction (with free bonus
commentary of the kind I share with writing & theology
students at genuine, expensive workshops!)*

I was seven years old when I penned—or penciled, actually—
my first work of fiction. It happened in a second-grade classroom, in December 1959, when my classmates and I were
ordered by kindly old Miss Hansen to make up and write
down a story about Christmas. Since most of us had only
been writing our names for a year or so, and only attempting
sentences for a few weeks, Miss Hansen left things pretty
wide open: we were free to babble about reindeer, snow-
men, Santa, Mrs. Santa, what we did or didn't want for
Christmas, whether we'd helped decorate the tree, you name
it. At age seven, though, I didn't just mess around: I set out
to write a completely original Christmas fiction, and made
the hero of my story Jesus Christ Himself.

My chief attraction to Jesus at that age was that, even
though He started out as a plain old little boy like me, He
grew up to become someone so mysterious and great that
my siblings and I were now being taught to pray to Him.
Talk about a Success! I tried to imagine my siblings or me

growing up to become somebody so great that other people prayed to us. Unthinkable!

A second thing that attracted me to Jesus at age seven: His father was allegedly God; and God had made the world and trees and rivers and stars and mountains and birds and clouds and sunlight and raspberries and animals and snow-flakes and wildflowers and wilderness; and even though nobody could prove any of this like, scientifically, I loved the world God had allegedly made so much that it seemed like a good idea to love God, too. Trouble was, I didn't. Loving Creation made sense to me the same way that lov-ing, say, Peanut M & M's made sense. You tossed a handful of Peanut M & M's in your mouth, crunched down, your tastebuds fired off, and without even trying, *Yum! Love! Gratitude!* Piece o' cake. Loving the Invisible God Who'd created Creation, on the other hand, felt more like trying to love the unknown and invisible people who worked at the Peanut M & M's factory.

This, I felt, was where Jesus came in. Because He'd been a regular little boy, then a less regular but still lovable man, there was somebody there to know. And knowing Jesus, in turn, was like knowing the son of somebody who worked at the Peanut M & M's factory. Without Him I pretty much drew a blank on who to thank for the many things for which I was grateful. Knowing Him put me in more of a *"Hey guy! Your dad makes great stuff!"* position. That's how I saw it at seven, anyway.

When I sat down to pen my Christmas story for Miss Hansen there were a few storytelling tools I lacked. On the writing side of the project, for instance, I wasn't yet sure what a quotation mark, paragraph, or comma was, and I'd never even heard of stuff like scene, plot, dialogue, irony, symbolism, metaphor. The one thing I knew about run-on sentences was that they sounded great to me. But I'd been literate for several months, I played baseball, I rode a bike. I figured I could drive a dang pencil across a page without crashing.

On the faith side of the project, similarly, there were some doctrinal issues I hadn't yet gotten on top of—and never would, as it's turned out. But I felt I knew the basics. I knew, for instance, that Jesus was born the year they started counting, on December 25th, o. I knew He was the son of a good Christian couple named Joseph and Mary, though the last name? Hmm. "Joseph and Mary Christ," was my best guess. I knew that Joseph was a carpenter, and that he taught his trade to Jesus, but that Jesus, like me, preferred fishing to carpentry—understandably, given the Cross! I knew that Joseph's claim to fame was his marriage to Mary—who was the only Virgin in the whole wide world, hence a miracle. I knew that Mary had lots of kids anyway, which was another miracle. The main thing was: I knew her eldest son, Jesus, was the biggest miracle of all, because of how He was God's son as well as Joseph's, in sort of the same way, I figured, that puppies or kittens can have more than one sire per litter.

This Multiple Dad concept was what triggered my christic fiction, actually. It fired my imagination, first of all, because my two older brothers were adopted and I wasn't. This really bugged me as a kid. When my parents would order my siblings and me to weed the garden or muck out the chicken house or rake the yard, my big brother John would set to work beside me, grumbling, "My *real* parents would never make me do this! My *real* parents are trapeze artists in the circus!"

You lucky bum! I'd think, because my *real* parents were the two utterly nontrapezian grumps who'd just put us to work. I figured that when Joseph, back in Bible times, doled out grunt chores to the Christ boys, Jesus could turn to his siblings the same way John turned to me and grouse, "My *real* Dad would never make me do this! My real Dad built the *Whole Universe!*"

My other fascination with the Multiple Dads concept had to do with birthday presents. What concerned me was that Jesus was a very good boy—the best boy ever, reputedly—and good boys deserve birthday presents. From *all* their fathers. But Jesus's heavy-duty Dad was either invisible, or living way up in heaven. So. How to get presents from an invisible or heavenly Father down to a deserving but earthbound son?

Solving this difficulty was my literary mission. My sense of the situation was that, even though Jesus was the Son of God, He was going to need some plain old human faith in order to locate a gift from His Invisible Father. If He slumped around the house on His birthday like some modern child of divorce, grumbling, "God is my real Dad, yeah. But big whip. 'Cause when is Invisible All-Powerful Dad gonna visibly remember my birthday?" I figured He was screwed from the get-go. But if, first thing birthday morn, He jumped up off the couch and went out alone into the part of the world that His Father had actually made and people hadn't yet wrecked—namely, wilderness—and if He walked around out there with an alert eye and a hopeful heart, then maybe good things could happen.

Since I didn't know what paragraphs were, my first short story turned out to be one stupendous paragraph long. Its title was supposed to be "Deborah," after a pretty girl I'd recently met in a picture book, but I somehow misremembered her "ah" as a "ha," spelled my title D-e-b-o-r-h-a, and pronounced it: "De-bore-HA."

My first and last christic fiction started like this:

It was the day before Christmas. Jesus was going to
be seven years old. He had fed all the animals but the
sheep. When he got to the fold one of the sheep were
gone its name was De-bore-HA. Jesus ran to his house
and ate his breakfast! . . .

(That last sentence, I must interrupt to say, is my favorite bit of fiction-making in the story. Check it out, young
writers: *Jesus ran to his house and ate his breakfast!* This
is a type of spontaneous detail that other writers about
Christ haven't yet dared to imagine. Not Kazantzakis; not
José Saramago; not Robert Graves; *certainly* not Norman
Mailer. I really captured something fresh here. I'm thinking I ought to pen an entire novel some day titled *Jesus
Ran to His House and Ate His Breakfast!* But on with our
story:)

Jesus ran to his house and ate his breakfast! Then he
went up in the mountains and looked for his lost sheep
calling De-bore-HA! De-bore-HA! He looked and
looked and at last he saw some wool on a bush. He
walked and walked and a little later said a prayer Dear
God please help me to find De-bore-HA Amen. [Nice
run-on, little David!] Then Jesus thought he knew
where to look. It was over in a pasture in another place
where a spring of water was. When he got there he saw
DE-BORE-HA! Oh De-bore-HA I have been so wor-
ried about you but just then he saw something moving.
De-bore-HA you have a baby lamb. Last year God
gave me a sparrow with a broken wing and this year
he gave me a lamb said Jesus . . .

(Sorry to interrupt again, but see how that trust-in-wilderness thing is working out? You sit home on your birthday watchin' the boob tube and waitin' for the mail lady, you end up getting adopted by the Prozac Family. But enter a little wilderness with an open eye and heart and *wham! Free lambs! Free sparrows! Direct-mailed from the Father!* That's how it's always worked for me, anyway.)

Okay. Up to here I had a good thing going. Even pronounced wrong, "De-bore-HA" was starting to give me an I-might-like-to-do-this-when-I-grow-up kind of feeling. But then came that Dark Night of the Literary Soul: the-problem-in-the-story-that-you-are-just-too-dumb-to-solve.

My plan was to send Jesus straight home with His baby lamb, let Him hang out with His miraculous mom, and the two of them would just chat a while as they celebrated His birthday. As I aimed my imagination in this direction, however, I could not for the life of me imagine what Jesus and Mary might sit around and chat about. I figured the topics would have to be Very Important, them being the Mother and Son of God. Maybe they'd chat up Jesus's importance as the advent of Christ, for example. But oh my hell. How to get Mary the Miraculous Virgin and Jesus the Christ Himself to sound natural and believable as they chatted about various Intergalactic Wonderments?

I was so daunted by this difficulty that I made poor Jesus sit there like a stick of furniture, not saying a word. Which left me Mary to work with. But what does the Virgin's chit-chat with her Savior Son sound like? I had No Idea.

In my decades of reading and writing since, I've learned that when panic-stricken authors have No Idea, they divide into two schools. One school summons a great false confidence to cover their doubt, and writes as if they're chiseling the words in marble. Were I of this school I'd have written:

LO, 'TIS I THE VIRGIN MARY
CHATTETHING WITH MY SON LORD
JESUS THE CHRIST, UPON THE EVENING
OF ONLY THE SEVENTH CHRISTMAS
IN ALL OF WORLD HISTORY! THIS IS
HOW I TALKETH, BY THE BY, AND
IF IT SOUNDETH PASSING STRANGE
OR UNREAL TO YOUR IGNORANT
AND UNWORTHY EARS YOU BETTER
BELIEVETH IN IT ANYHOW, BUSTER,
BECAUSE I AM ONE IMPORTANT LADY!

The other school of panic-stricken writers try to avoid thinking altogether. Instead, they drink four or five cups of coffee or a pint of whiskey as they stare at the blank page, then explode in a burst of word jazz they hope readers will mistake for early Kerouac. This was my approach. My Jesus and Mary birthday scene went:

When he got home he remembered Mary his mother
had promised to tell Jesus the story of when he was
born Mary said one day I was cleaning house our
angel came to me and said go to Bethlehem there you
will have a baby his name is to be Jesus. So we went to
Bethlehem. When we got there that night we were very
tired the inn was full but the inn keeper was nice so he
let us go in the stable for the night and there Jesus was
born. Angels sang and told the shepherds to go to the
stable where Jesus was born. There was a big star in the

sky and the wise men came and gave Jesus some thing
made of gold. Then the angels came again and here we
are. That night Jesus and Mary saw a star almost as
big as the one in Bethlehem for the first Christmas.

End of paraphraph. End of feeble fledgling of a story.
And the whole experience would remain as forgettable as
the story—were it not for a small miracle that occurred as
I wrote:

Goofy as my story was, as soon I started telling it I vanished. The classroom did too. So did the other kids. And
that vanishing. Lost in the doing. Ego gone. What happens
when this happens? Who are we when we're gone? This
mystery has shone at the heart of my love for fiction writing
from the moment Jesus ran to His house and ate His breakfast. Flannery O'Connor said: "No art is sunk in the self, but
rather, in art the self becomes self-forgetful in order to meet
the demands of the thing seen and the thing being made."
W. H. Auden said: "To pray is to pay attention to something
or someone other than oneself. Whenever a man so concen-
trates his attention—on a landscape, a poem, a geometrical
problem, an idol, or the True God—that he completely for-
gets his own ego and desires, he is praying." Though "De-
bore-HA" fell to ruin at the end, it haunted me that, once
I sank into the work, a half-embodied desert wilderness
and approximation of the boy Jesus took my classmates'
and classroom's places. I loved both halves of this magic:
my own disappearance; the desert's and boy's appearances.
I loved it so much I suspected it might be related to the loss
Jesus refers to when He says, "He that loseth his life shall
save it." As near as I can tell, the moment I disappeared that
morning is the moment that O'Connor's "art" and Auden's
"prayer" were destined to become my life's work.

As a teacher I have since come to recommend to working writers that we engage in this loss of self in private, however, for when we vanish into the making of our art, it turns out, our bodies do not vanish with us. I learned this the hard way in Miss Hansen's class. I grew so lost that I failed to notice when every student but me finished their story and passed it up to Miss H; next I failed to notice a few students, then everyone in the room, turning to watch me madly scribbling; I then failed to notice them bottling their mirth and letting me work undisturbed as Miss Hansen strolled up the aisle, stopped by my desk, crossed her arms, maybe tapped a toe, maybe cleared her throat. When even then I labored on, the kids exploded, flying me from the Holy Land back into an ego and an East Portland, Oregon, classoom in an instant.

Crimson-faced, I handed Miss H my story. Because of my monumental absorption, she read it on the spot. As she did so, her face took on a dangerously thrilled look. She then nearly killed my Call-to-Writing in the hour of its birth—by bending down and kissing me, right there in front of God and everybody. Thus did I learn that reviews, positive or negative, are the hardest thing about this gig for me.

When Miss Hansen later got "Deborha" published in a countywide anthology of kids' writings, though, I had to admit that, reviews notwithstanding, I kinda liked seeing my personal disappearances and characters' appearances wandering the countryside in print.

I still do. So I keep disappearing.

Romeo Shows Jamey the Door

Preface

I know of three couples whose relationships lasted almost exactly as long as the life of each couple's dog. Oddly, all three couples included a writer, and all three dogs were border collies. The trios were Barry Lopez, his ex-wife Sandra, and their dog Desert; the poet Jane Hirshfield, her ex-partner Michael, and their dog Maggie; and I, my ex-wife Alice, and our dog Hafiz Pancake. (A hafiz, by the way, is a man who has memorized the entire Koran. Hafiz Pancake was a dog who'd memorized the fact that he loved my homemade buttermilk pancakes.)

Not long after a divorce decree euthanized my first marriage, I held Pancake in my lap while a vet did the same for him. At the instant of death, I was unexpectedly jerked out of sorrow by something rationalists will consider impossible. Paul Auster speaks to this kind of impossibility when he writes, "A thing that isn't there is there." W.B. Yeats does the same when he writes, "There is another world, but it is in this one." The Tibetan Buddhist scholar Robert Thurman goes even Yeats one better. In *Circling the Sacred Mountain,* Thurman writes: "All beings are. They never are not. They are either alive or between. There is, hypothetically, a split second between life and the between that is properly called death. A boundary, a line with no width, something ultimately not there except as an arbitrary border."

Holding my steadfast old dog up to and through the instant he left his body, I somehow glimpsed this border. The experience was beautiful beyond words, and it transformed for good the way I hear the term "border collie."

When I later tried to write of the experience, I ran into a familiar wall: the event had not really been *personal*, it had been spiritual, and only the spirit has spiritual experiences. So when the limited "I" tries to write of such experiences the soul and mystery of them vanish and what remains are what Merton calls "itsty-bitsy statues" of a spiritual experience.

I abandoned my attempt. Years passed. Then one day, while I was lost in the effort to create a long work of fiction, a character in my story unexpectedly, almost effortlessly underwent the very experience that I, as an "I," had been unable to capture at all.

The pages that follow are that fragment, and I may never polish, expand, or weave it into anything. No matter, I think. I'd still like to let this shard of fiction share its nonfictitious glimpse of eternity via the death of a marvelous dog.

Romeo Shows Jamey the Door

Love, and a bit with a dog. That's what they want.

THE THEATER MANAGER,

SHAKESPEARE IN LOVE

On March 1, 2000, the Portland actor and playwright Jamey Van Zandt held his best friend in his arms, nodded to the doctor standing over them, then watched that doctor, in obedience to his nod, end his friend's life with a lethal injection.

This world being a cauldron of war, violent separation, murders, sudden injuries, and suffering, it's anticlimactic to admit that this friend was just a black-and-tan border collie named Romeo. But it's true. Jamey loved a lot of people a little, and a few people a lot, but in duration of intimacy he'd been closer to Romeo than to any human he'd ever lived with, and even in *degree* of intimacy he'd been closer to Romeo than to anyone but his wife, Risa. Romeo spent seventeen years glued to Jamey's side, incessantly and non-judgmentally imbibing his master's most intimate moods and odors; seventeen years jumping up out of sleep just to dog Jamey's random pacing during wee-hour insomnia attacks. Risa and Jamey were close but not the way Romeo and Jamey were. Risa did not spend her formative years sleeping on Jamey's feet. When Jamey was attending college classes she did not lie upon his rancid old tennis shoe in the hall outside because that shoe was the one thing on earth that would keep her from howling. She did not insist, every morning, on following Jamey to lie outside the locked bathroom as he moved his bowels. Nor did she greet him when he opened the door, greet him *thousands of times in a row*, with grins and tail wags of such ecstatically congratulatory delight that Jamey by God came to feel he really *had* accomplished something wonderful in there.

For seventeen years Romeo shared his master's solitudes and social chaos, his inertias and manias, his voluntary maledictions, involuntary prayers, his worst, his best, his everything. These two were no duo. They were a six-legged man/dog unit so incessantly linked that most people found them absurd at first. But after years would pass and they'd bump into the Jamey/Romeo Unit again, something would flip like an egg over easy inside them and the absurd would become the Exemplary. Yes, Romeo was just a dog. But for seventeen years he watched over Jamey's erratic incarnation with keenest interest, yet without judgment—the way poor old Jesus once recommended we all watch over one another. Romeo's love for his master came within a single condition of attaining that godlike level known as "unconditional." What's more, the sole condition to Romeo's love was simply his wish that Jamey never leave his sight.

So that's who, on March 1, 2000, Jamey held in his arms. That's whose brown eyes he gazed into, then turned from, to nod to the doctor. That was the life, the friend, the part of himself, he then watched die via lethal injection.

The adventures of the six-legged Jamey/Romeo Unit would fill a thousand pages. Only one such adventure funnels into the mystery I want to ponder here. It concerns a door.

In the forty-first chapter of the book of Job, the poet, in

pondering the Almighty, asks: "*Who can open the doors of His face?*"

My favorite response to this is Emerson's: "*There is a crack in everything God has made.*"

As his parting gift to his friend and master, Romeo showed Jamey just such a crack—the very crack, so Jamey believes, that serves the soul as door, offering a deathless exit out of the otherwise airtight world in which God has fatally encased us.

Jamey is no mystic. There is, he insists, no woowoo in his experience. He says that Romeo, as a parting gift, answered Job 41's question by literally opening a door in this world's face and showing Jamey a way out. "The door was palpable," he says. "Invisible but physical. I heard and felt it. It was real."

To preface the door, all that really need be said is that for seventeen years Romeo and Jamey comprised a comic yet beautiful Union, but that somehow, Jamey never could quite understand it, Romeo grew old while Jamey did not, despite their beautiful Union. The dog's teeth became useless nubs. His sight and hearing faded. His sleek fur grew drab and, to put it modestly, doggy-smelling. Chronic arthritis turned his front paws into something more like flippers. The drugs for the arthritis attacked and weakened his heart.

There is a sidehill yard, with a large cement goldfish pond, behind Risa and Jamey's Northwest Portland apartment house. In exchange for maintaining this pond and yard, Jamey purchased lavatorial and exercise rights for Romeo in the azaleas above the pond. One frigid winter morning Jamey let the dog out to use his beshrubbed bathroom, whistled for him a half hour later, then walked out to see why the dog didn't come. He found that Romeo's hips had collapsed, sending him sideways down the little hill into the ice-rimmed pond, where he now stood, submerged to the neck, too arthritic to climb out. But because Jamey had long since forbidden Romeo to bark in the morning, lest he wake all the neighbors, the dog remained silent. Unable to move, dying of hypothermia, he would have stood in the icy water, refusing to break his master's command till his spirit left him.

Within two days of this episode Romeo developed a sinus infection that grew chronic. The recommended drugs didn't cure the infection, but they did make Romeo incontinent. Mortification at every indoor mistake was now as palpable in his eyes as his love. He began to sneeze, convulsively, trying to clear the infected sinuses, but his arthritis had destroyed his ability to control the sneezes, so he'd accidentally smash his muzzle on the floor, giving himself profuse nosebleeds. These too mortified him. The pawprints Risa and Jamey would find when they'd get home from work showed how Romeo hobbled round and round the apartment, trying between sneezes to lick up all the blood he kept spilling.

The downward spiral went on for months. Risa was a saint about it, never once suggesting the dog be put down. "We've been together four years," she told Jamey. "You and Romeo have been together seventeen. He's your call." In marriage, though, nothing belongs to just one person. Jamey did all the cleanup when he was home, but when he wasn't, Risa dealt with every incontinence without complaint.

The beginning of the end didn't come till Risa and Jamey's fifteen-month-old daughter, Lilly, was given one of those leg-propelled, bumper-car-like contraptions toddlers use to learn to walk. Lilly grew adept at it, then downright reckless, one day ramming the thing into a deep-asleep Romeo. He lurched up and grabbed her shin. Just a warning grab. But one old fang, broken off to a point years before, pierced Lilly and drew blood.

Even then Risa made no ultimatums. But Romeo himself was so mortified that he refused, for weeks afterward, to leave the big tuba-case Jamey had long ago turned into his doggy bed—except to have more accidents, or to sneeze, bang his muzzle, bleed.

The time had come.

As Romeo's namesake finally put it,

> Let me have a dram of poison, such soon-speeding
> gear as will disperse itself through all the veins,
> that the life-weary taker may fall dead, and that
> the trunk may be discharged of breath as violently
> as hasty powder fired doth hurry from the fatal
> cannon's womb.

In the tiny Oregon coast town of Hebo, a college pal of Risa's—a laconic Chinese American named Gai Li—was the practicing large animal vet. Three weeks after the bite, seeing Romeo still in his bed, Jamey quietly asked Risa to phone Gai.

Gai told her, "Have Jamey bring the dog before we open at eight tomorrow."

Jamey chose Gai and the coast for a reason. An hour south of Hebo, a storm-smashed, basaltic headland juts out into the Pacific. This was the place where Jamey and his sister, Judith, had scattered their mother's ashes when they were five and seven years old. Jamey and Romeo had hiked the headland every summer for seventeen years. The most beautiful, haunted place he knew was the only place Jamey could imagine leaving this dog behind for good.

At 4:30 A.M. on March 1, Jamey slipped a fold-up Army shovel into the bed of his Toyota truck, loaded the tuba-case dog bed, then whistled for the dog.

When Romeo came prancing, eagerly and at once, St. Risa finally lost it. Her sobs, as she hugged Romeo good-bye, made him feel confused and guilty. Which made Risa sob harder. "It's not your fault, it's not your fault!" she kept gasping.

Which made Lilly start to cry. Which made Romeo look as if even he were crying. Which made Lilly start to laugh. Which cheered Risa and Romeo back up.

Jamey grabbed Romeo quickly, set him on the front passenger seat, and drove away fast while it still seemed re-motely possible.

As Romeo rode toward the coast in his old shotgun po-sition, he seemed to grow younger by the mile. Risa had displaced him in this seat of honor years ago. Much as he loved Risa, he resumed his old place with a look of smug vindication.

They reached Hebo in three hours. Jamey located the Large Animal Clinic, then drove, as prearranged, around back, parking in a spruce-lined, mist-shrouded meadow. Romeo took one look at the meadow and began blissfully panting in anticipation of a hike. Then Gai Li stepped out the back door, "drams" and "soon-speeding gear" at the ready.

Romeo's pant changed to one of fear. Though he'd never set eyes on Gai, he recognized Risa's friend at once for what he was: a damned animal doctor. Jamey felt sick, as Gai approached, to think that Romeo's distrust of vets had been prophetic all along. And mortality was not even the source of Romeo's fear. Vets had twice saved his life, once from salmon fever, once from a poisoned deer carcass. In so doing, however, they'd committed the unforgivable sin: they had separated Romeo from his master.

Fear lent Romeo its strange strength. While Jamey greeted and thanked Gai, and paid him in advance, the dog trotted off across the meadow to a huge Sitka spruce, did his spryest leglift in years, then beamed his inimitable smile back at Jamey as if to say, *See? Limber as can be! Strong stream! Pleasant-smelling, too! No need for vets! I'm fine and dandy.*

Jamey wished Romeo would just wander into the mist, leaving him with this image forever.

Wishing accomplished the usual nothing. And when the dog cantered back to Jamey, his tail now wagging despite the presence of Gai, Jamey grew so nauseous with the sense of betrayal that he half collapsed into the wet grass.

While Gai watched in silence, Jamey gruffly ordered Romeo to lie down beside him.

Romeo hadn't disobeyed Jamey yet. Turned out he never would.

Jamey slid Romeo's body—suddenly old and painfully knotted again—onto his lap.

The dog panted hard, kept an eye on Gai, but tried to smile up at Jamey, too, grateful for this awkward but rare intimacy.

Gai said, "Ready?"

Jamey clamped a hand round Romeo's muzzle to prevent a bite.

Gai slipped a tourniquet around Romeo's foreleg, located a vein, produced the sedative syringe from his green lab coat pocket, calmly remarked, "This is the relaxer," and drove the fluid into Romeo's bloodstream before Jamey or Romeo could fully take it in.

An instant later the fatal syringe was in Gai's hand, already poised.

Loathing the man's efficiency, but recognizing the desperate lateness of his and Romeo's united, six-legged life, Jamey gazed down into the dog's brown eyes, put his theatrical training fiercely to work, drove Gai from his mind, and made Romeo alone his focus.

He couldn't bear to say, "It's gonna be all right." He couldn't bear to say anything. But as he gazed at Romeo the words *unforgivable mercy* floated into his head and stayed there. An odd-sounding concept. Yet there it lay in his lap, still adoring him, still beautiful despite his fear.

Gai glanced the final question.

Romeo panted hard, but kept his eyes locked on Jamey's.

Without a glance at Gai, staying faithful to their eyelock, Jamey nodded.

In went the syringe.

Actor that he was, Jamey's calm appeared perfect as he asked, "Will it be fast?" But when Gai answered, "Very," something amorphous and black rose up in Jamey's chest and flopped over in a spilled heap. And whatever that black thing is, Jamey says, it'll never leave. He says it's flopped over and spilled in him, still.

Yet Romeo kept on panting. *He kept on panting!* Jamey tried not to run with this; tried not to pray that Gai had underdosed him, maybe grabbed the wrong syringe; tried not to picture himself saying, "Well, we gave it a shot, Romeo, but fuck this! Let's go home!"

Gai even began, to Jamey's joy, to look slightly panicked.

Then came the snap.

Jamey felt it throughout Romeo's body.

And that's what the snap made of him: a body: a dog no more.

But a split second, split eternity, split hair after the snap, or maybe simultaneous to the snap but *deep inside it,* Jamey felt something in the atoms that comprise the very wall of this world: felt it with his whole being, including body and mind.

Who can open the doors of His face? asks the Job poet. But the question is rhetorical—a faith statement in disguise. The poet is certain that the only possible answer is an awed: "*No one.*"

Yet at the instant of death, instant of the snap, Romeo, Jamey, and a third body they'd built through seventeen years of intimacy, discovered something. Simultaneous to the nervous system recoil that ended their united life, Jamey felt a perfectly crafted, airtight door open, felt his friend shoot silently through, felt the door close,

tk!

felt the slight suction of its closing.

And a thing that wasn't there was there.

Jamey was transported. What struck him first was the impossible door's perfect minimalist beauty. What he sensed as Romeo left him was the most exquisitely crafted device imaginable—because *there was nothing to it.* Death's door, as he experienced his closest friend darting through, was the handiwork of an aesthetic so sublimely minimal that the artifact supposedly created by it—death itself—wasn't even there. The body, abandoned in a split second, was now dead matter. And the beloved being was gone with an ease so total it left being intact: *tk!*

Gone into a what? As what? Gone where? Who knew? Legends and scriptures abounded, and Jamey would now read them with a fresh-opened mind. In defiance of every expectation he'd had, the shooting away of Romeo's life struck him as *a perfect work of the Unseen's art.* To feel the opening and closing of death's door was to touch the very carpentry of the Invisible. Nothing to see. Nothing to hold on to afterward but an emptied dog. Yet Jamey felt certain, after the *tk!* and tiny suction, that his dog had indeed been emptied, that the being he loved had departed intact, and that this world was no longer the only world: it was one of a now-accessible two: the darker, sadder one, with singing thrushes, cold mist, and beautiful, shaggy old evergreens in it.

Gazing at this world's trees—gazing at the very spruce Romeo's blithe piss still warmed—Jamey's jaw went slack and he was a child again, hunched on a rug with his sister Jude, looking at their dead mother's elaborate old wooden advent calendar, with twenty-five camouflaged Countdown Doors hiding ever-greater gifts behind the world wall. Staring at the spruce, the meadow, the mist between, Jamey felt the gift he'd called Romeo hovering behind an advent wall of trees and water vapor, intact in every way that counted, the feel of his hidden smile traveling back through a crack to Jamey. And the solaces grew so vast they defeated grief. Holding Romeo's cooling body in his lap, Jamey was awash in the same pure wonder he'd felt when Lilly's tiny body, fully formed and perfect, slid into this world from a realm whose advent door had, preposterously, been Risa. He hadn't understood then. He didn't understand now. He just sensed, without understanding, that the darting of Romeo's life out of this world was not the opposite of Lilly's birth, but its twin. Whatever or whoever made Romeo Romeo was no more dead than was Lilly in the moments before her birth.

When the hand-dug grave was filled and a tiny Sitka spruce planted in the broken soil, Jamey found himself suddenly two-leggèd, black clouds rolled in over solace, and he needed to sob himself to exhaustion and cry himself utterly dry.

Yet the word "death," the once fierce skeptic insists to this day, can never again mean "end of story." Thanks to a four-leggèd moon that for seventeen years circled the planet of his body, the word for Jamey now means,

tk!

And the door's openings and closings—hard to countenance and mysterious as they remain—have not felt purely bitter ever since.

11

✦ ✦ ✦ ✦ ✦ ✦ ✦

Are Salmon Holy?

A couple of years ago I published a darned-near meta-physical collection of nonfiction, called *My Story as Told by Water*, about my lifelong love for rivers, fly-fishing, and most especially, wild salmon. When the book won awards, then a throng of fishing dweebs, river guardians, earth muffins, conservationists, and even a few priests and theologians began to sing its praises, the religion editor of one of the Northwest's largest newspapers noticed. She contacted the Portland writer of faith and freelance interviewer, Brian Doyle, and told him that some fella named Duncan was crisscrossing the country preaching that salmon are essential to the Pacific Northwest's chain of life, economy, mental stability, Christian integrity, and culture.

"I know the man," said Brian Doyle.

When the editor complained of my claim that a diet of wild salmon will cure mental illness, unite the human heart with all of nature, and inspire cold-turkey abstinence from network TV and partisan politics, Brian remarked, "Too bad salmon's seasonal."

When she said that I get on a high horse—that, for example, I call salmon "divine gifts created in an unend-ing Beginning," and "a product less of evolution than of unconditional love"—Brian replied, "He's a Scot, a people famous for strong stances. They flavor their whiskeys with dirt. They fish with seventeen-foot rods. The men wear skirts. They eat haggis for god's sake. But they do love their sacred salmon. Maybe it's love that makes Duncan's horse so high."

Brian's profound grasp of the Scots is rooted in his Irishness. The Irish make their whiskeys out of spud lymph. They kiss an unhygienic stone for luck. They play their pipes with their armpits. They're too busy scraping fiddles to fish with any length of rod. Their men don't wear kilts, but their women wear the pants. They envy the Scots terribly. But they're our next-door neighbors and first cousins, and love the salmon as we do. So when the editor hired Brian to interview me for her paper, I was happy.

The question we were to debate, the religion editor told Brian, was whether it is theologically accurate to say that wild salmon are holy. The trouble with this plan was, I've spent thousands of days on rivers awestruck and in love with the very holiness she wished to see "debated." Barring amnesia, debate is not possible for a man so sculpted: my river-born certainty as to the holiness of salmon long ago achieved the sort of vehemence we associate with Old Testament prophets.

Indeed, upon learning of our topic I asked Brian, who's Catholic, if he were well enough connected in Rome to get my views on salmon's holiness published in some obscure corner of the Bible. "Where might we sneak it in, do you think?" asked Brian.

"Joshua, Judges, Ruth, Samuel, Kings, Coho?" I suggested.

"The few who notice may object," said he.

"Subtlety then," I whispered. "Nahum, Habakkuk, Humpback, Zephaniah."

"Could be we've missed the deadline," said Brian.

"Rome saints new saints," I argued. "They can sign off on a Song of Salmon. I'll pen it gratis. I promise to be inspired. I'll wear a crimson beanie while I write. Think of it! A Book of Chinook in the Holy Bible! The legislation we'd pass! The restoration funds we'd raise!"

"The daily paper must do for today," said Brian.

So began an interview that, according the religion editor, would have stood out in her paper like a fresh-caught fifty-pound chinook would stand out were it thrashing on the floor of the New York Stock Exchange. Our conversation had to be expurgated to protect a readership more comfortable with natural disasters, murders, wars, and the like. But in a book intended, like this one, for true Christians, which is of course to say salmon lovers, our unedited talk could be just what the doctor ordered. So here's a sample:

Brian Doyle: Tell me why folks who don't care about salmon extinction and salmon restoration should care about them.

DJD: Some people are just emotionally disabled and short-circuited and non compos mentis, God bless them and keep them. But for a mentally competent resident of the Pacific Northwest, to say "I don't care about the extinction of wild salmon" is like saying "I don't care about the history of my home, the health of my home, or the death of the cultures, lifeways, jobs, flora and fauna of my home." It's like saying you don't care about the preservation of the Northwest's greatest source of food ever—a source of healthful marine protein that, over the course of millennia, has fed more people than all the Northwest's beef and dairy cattle, wheat, corn, and lentils combined. To say you don't care about the disappearance of salmon is like saying you don't care, despite living in a democracy, about the will of the people, a vast majority of whom proclaim passionate willingness to resurrect dying salmon runs. It's like saying you don't care whether your government obeys life-giving laws like the Endangered Species Act and Clean Water Act. It's like saying you don't care whether our leaders keep our endlessly broken treaties with still-living, still-deserving, still-financially-cheated Indian tribes, though the salmon are the Eucharist and life's blood of these sovereign people. It's like saying you don't care about European heritage, either—your own Irish heritage for instance, Brian. (*"Cairill, King of Ulster, took me in his net. Ah, that was a happy man when he saw me! He shouted for joy when he saw the great salmon in his net."*) Saying you don't care about salmon, I'm sorry to say, is more or less like confessing that you're lost in a self-absorbed consumer stupefaction that won't end till the Northwest's Chain of Life is doomed and your children's children with it. So I pray, for your soul's sake, that you say and think no such thing.

Brian Doyle: Whoa!

DJD: Sorry. You asked.

Brian: So how is a wild chinook salmon the size of your leg a holy creature?

DJD: Because *"God said, Let the waters bring forth abundantly the moving creature that hath life. . . . And God created great whales, and every living creature that moveth, which the waters brought forth abundantly, after their kind, and every winged fowl after his kind: and God saw that it was good. And God blessed them, saying, Be fruitful, and multiply, and fill the waters in the seas."* Salmon are holy because *"the Earth is the Lord's, and the fullness thereof"* (Psalms), and because *"everything shall live whither the river cometh . . . and the fish shall be exceed-*

ing many . . . and ye shall inherit them, one as well as another"
(Ezekiel), and because we humans are mere *"tenants"* on this
earth (Leviticus), placed here as *"caretakers"* (Genesis), and
the great guide of Christian caretakers was a fisherman who
advised a dominion that rules God's planet not as self-serving industrialists would have it, but *"on earth as it is in heaven"*
(Matthew, Luke), as the Lord would have it.

As a huge fan of the gospels I must add that when
salmon feed their young bodies to kingfishers and otters and
eagles, and their larger oceangoing bodies to seals, sea lions,
orcas, and their magnificent, sexually driven, returned-to-
the-river bodies to bears and Indian tribes and sport fishers and fly fishers, then even their spawned-out bodies to
salmonberries, swordferns, cedar trees, mosses and wildflowers, they have served us, from one end of their lives
to the other, as a kind of living gospel themselves. When a
salmon's nitrogen-rich body feeds trees and flowers, it is literally "considering the lilies of the field." When its flesh feeds
even the most intractable salmon haters among us, they are
literally "loving their enemies and doing good to those who
hate them." Wild chinook the size of my leg—well, not my
leg, my legs are kinda skinny—but damned big salmon of all
six species have forever climbed our rivers like the heroes of
a wondrous Sunday sermon, nailing their shining bodies to
lonely beds of gravel not for anything they stand to gain, but
that tiny silver offspring and three hundred salmon-eating
species of flora and fauna may live and thrive. When these
blessings no longer come, the Northwest's living image of
self-sacrifice goes silent: no more sermon. As the father of
three kids to whom I'd love to pass down the faith that their
hearts are heroic and their souls immortal, I find the silence
of salmonless rivers very hard to bear.

Brian Doyle: More about that. What are the thousand rivers, cricks, and rivulets of the Great Northwest without salmon and steelhead in them? Tell me the shape of their vast emptiness.

DJD: The emptiness that hits me hardest, having lived near salmon streams all my life, is the spiritual void, after the salmon run's extinction, in the lives of the resident humans. Any person waist deep in a misty green river, casting for salmon, is in a position of prayerfulness. He or she is hoping to defy the odds, hook a Genesis gift, beach it, bless it, and bring it home to wow and feed the friends and family. Such a person is an indigenous being of an ancient sort, a being known as a fisher. It's worth mentioning that never, in a salmonless future, will any conceivable Northwest Christ have this trade from which to draw apostles as He did in Galilee. As a fisher myself, I owe it to Peter, James, and John to try to safeguard our line of work.

When the thousand rivers and rills are stripped of salmon, the tribes' cultural bankruptcy and fishing ports' bankruptcies and kids' and river otters' and birds' and seals' and cedar trees' and bears' and wildflowers' bankruptcies dovetail into a great desolation and dearth the Northwest's Catholic bishops rightly call "a tragedy of the sacred commons." When the rivers are stripped by ignorance, greed or apathy, even great salmon-spirited cities like Seattle are stripped of their connection to nature, their rites of seasonal mystery, their culture. You don't go down to Pike Place Market for the joy of purchasing a thin strip of Gorton-brand® scrod. And what, football fans, do genuine "seahawks" clutch in their talons at sea? What, baseball fans, swims beneath actual "mariners" on the actual waves? When the rivers are stripped of salmon our identities are stripped, posterity is stripped, unborn childen are stripped, all humanity is stripped of a spiritual compass bearing and a means of livelihood as ancient as prayer.

And what becomes of us then, Brian my friend? One of the great proofs of salmons' holiness is what becomes of people deprived of them. When I see some raggedy-ass gambler in a riverside casino with a liquid addiction in one hand and a smoke in the other, shoving quarters into a poker machine, defying loan sharks and ruin in hopes of bringing a little wow into his life, I think, *There, but for industrial greed and Satan, stands a fisherman.* That man is 3-D proof of the emptiness of the thousand rills and cricks. Without the river's great gift he's a coho at the mouth of a dewatered stream, his heart circling and circling, unable to find his way home.

So I say *Proverbs, Ecclesiastes, Song of Solomon, Song of Salmon forever!* As Peter, James, and John are surely shouting down from heaven, we need these silver gifts in our rivers, bellies, and hearts to inspire Galilean-spirited, courageous, self-giving Northwest lives.

Brian Doyle: Amen and then again, amen.

Christian Matters II

an Image *magazine conversation with Doug Thorpe*
conducted in 2001, excised for this book by DJD

IMAGE: It strikes me as curious how often individuals who appear to have "fallen away" from "the fold" have in fact fallen more deeply into love with the divine. I'm thinking, for example, of Chaim Potok, whose novel *My Name Is Asher Lev* describes the experience of a boy growing up to be an artist, and ultimately losing his family and spiritual community (Hasidic) even while his absolute devotion to his God-given art is seen within the novel as a fulfillment of the Hasidic call to devotion to God. I'm thinking also of many of my friends and students, whose devotion to the truth in their lives is viewed by family and community as a violation of their own beliefs. Was this in some way your experience? If so, how did you make the crossing into a kind of faith that can embrace Rumi and salmon as easily as Jesus?

DJD: My best answer to that question is a thousand pages of fiction called *The River Why* and *The Brothers K.* But I'll give you a shorter answer if you, in return, will agree to steer us away from theology in a while. Deal?

IMAGE: Deal.

DJD: I was forced as a boy to attend both Seventh-day Adventist and Presbyterian "institutions of worship." My mother and grandma did it out of love—but also out of a paranoia carefully engendered in good people by bad preachers everywhere. I found both institutions nonsensical, but disliked the Presbyterian institution more, for its lukewarm banality. The SDAs, in contrast, were as passionate and nutty as a buncha squirrels. The vegetarianism, no makeup, no jewelry. The no dancing. (Boy are there some raunchy jokes I could tell about that!) The Friday-sunset-to-Saturday-sunset Sabbath. And those old Adventist sermons! Zowie! They made every Sabbath a small Halloween, only it was "Paradise or Perdition" instead of "trick or treat." Unlike most Protestant churches, the SDAs protected their boys from the Vietnam War. I'll always love 'em for that. On the other hand, if the preachers of my youth are correct, all you Sunday worshippers are going to hell for all eternity. This isn't a very loving point of view, and I personally find it rather untenable (though anything's possible!). So when the time came, I happily fled the whole wacky little extravaganza.

I continue to distrust and reject Christian fundamentalism and televangelism, not because they're "all wrong," but because they seem to me to do more harm than good. The chief problem is the arrogance of folks who think that in possessing a book, a dogma, the letter of a Law, they possess the Truth. For me, love is the truth and the expression of love, in any form, is allegiance to Christ. Love, as I see it, is nondogmatic, essentially self-giving, and endlessly sensitive to the needs, nuances, and happiness of others. Most dogmatists, on the other hand, believe they're the Chosen People, and that it's their duty, while "marching as to war" with a "Mighty Fortress" of a "God," to browbeat the rest of us into embracing the same close-minded Chosenness, or else become Other. The logical outcome of the various fundamentalisms is an endless series of holy wars to decide who is the most truly "chosen." No fundamentalism is capable of loving its neighbors, let alone its enemies. What's more, in Matthew, chapters 6 and 7, Jesus lists about twenty attributes of fundamentalists and evangelists as examples of how not to live a life. You won't hear Pat Robertson quoting Matthew 6:5 on TV, for example.

The Baptist sage Will Campbell calls televangelists "electronic soul-molesters." I like the justified revulsion in this comment, but as a believer in the Vedantic *atma* I feel that the soul, though capable of being smothered, is ultimately unmolestable. Televangelists remind me more of people who, on a cold dark night, when you're huddled up by a small, carefully tended, soulful little campfire, drag over thirteen plaster statues of Jesus and the Apostles and a fourteenth bronze statue of that fine old sexist, St. Paul, plus a three-ton titanium-covered edition of the Americanized and bowdlerized and reified Metallic Bible, and throw them all on your little fire, smothering the flames. As you huddle in the dark, freezing your ass off, the televangelist defends his effrontery by claiming it's the plaster statues and Metal Bible you need, not your life-giving fire. He then pulls out an offering plate and asks you to pay him for what he's done.

To my mind, the proper response to all such requests is: *Hahahahaha! You have GOT to be kidding!* Seriously, I believe it's a form of credulity close to sin to give money to anybody who asks for it in the name of Jesus or God—Billy Graham, the Catholic Church, anybody. It encourages intense illusion and hypocrisy. Better to tell the people asking for such money to get a *real* job. Think of the misery Pat Robertson will have to endure in his next life if we're so stupid as to pay him as he "prays on street corners" claiming to represent Jesus Himself! Face it, Pat: the known and unknown universes are God's! He hardly needs this green-backed shite we call money. It's you and your propaganda machine that need our money.

If Jesus appeared among us as an ordinary man today, would He watch TV? Would He watch Pat's show? Would He be an "institutional Christian"? Was He an institutional Jew, a proud scribe, a proud Pharisee? Jesus's response to the religion of His day is a major clue to His likely response to the religion of our day. That's why I believe that, if Jesus walked the earth today, the famous televangelists, after being scandalized by Him, would fit Him neatly into their Metallic Bible-worship under the heading "false christ," and reject Him. The Jesus fundamentalist patriarchs worship lives either up in the sky, or in the Holy Land two thousand years ago. In other words: at a safe distance. Not here on earth. Not *now* on earth.

Here and now on earth, if the Jesus I believe in ran into a freezing person by a tiny fire on a cold night, He would sit down so close beside that person that their bodies would begin to warm each other. And if Jesus had a fundamentalist's Unerring Bible with Him, and the warmth of His body wasn't enough to fend off the stranger's hypothermia, He'd burn that Bible for warmth.

IMAGE: How is it that you escaped from the fold without a dogmatic bone in your body? And—at least it seems—without much bitterness?

DJD: My bones and I are dogmatic as hell! Just not about religion. Frankly, religion doesn't much interest me. Spirituality, yes. Religion, no. That's why we need to change the subject soon. But I do dogmatically believe that the fly reel should be placed on the rod with the handle to the right, British style, not to the left, spinning-rod style, and that trout fishing clothes must be dark and preferably green in color—like the Holy Prophet's handsome green turban— and that the best fishing guide is the Islamic Holy Ghost, *al-Khizr*. I also dogmatically hold that tea should not be oversteeped, and that honey and cream should be added to avoid kidney stones, and that the literary impulse, including my own to write novels, is better fed by poetry and myth than by contemporary novels, and that television is evil even when the program is good because it pacifies, stupefies, and isolates, and that the Cross is inescapable whether you're ensconced in a "fold" or not, and that Norman Maclean was a better theologian than Billy Graham, and that Nepotism is president, and that Gary Snyder will go down in Spiritual History as a far more influential leader than Clinton or either Bush, because he was never elected to public office, and knows what "is" is, and when speaking in public makes up his own words out of his own depths, not scripted words spawned by some sleazeball's conniving. I dogmatically believe, furthermore, that diehard baseball fans are wiser about the object of their adoration than the average diehard bishop is about the object of his, and that Catholicism is a second-rate religion because they won't saint Meister Eckhart, or pray for the recovery of the Beguines they exterminated, or undo their fifth-century condemnation of reincarnation and Origen, or ordain women, or appoint women bishops, or (DREAM BIG!) elect a woman pope. But I also believe that Protestantism, by comparison, is a third-rate religion, the gradual effect of which has been to divide Christendom into billions of "denominations," each with a membership of one, each with its own whacked translation of the Bible, every man his own pope—and a spiritual leader named

David James the First strikes me as incomparably more horrific than John Paul the Second, so of the two religions, Catholicism and Protestantism, I slightly prefer the former, but happily choose Comedy, such as you are reading, over either.

As for my having left institutional religion behind without bitterness: how in the Name of the Lover of field lilies, the poor, the prostituted, and His own murderers, could I be bitter about having traded self-righteousness, pharisaism, judgmentalism, and church pews for sunlit river banks and rising fish and moonrises over Rocky Mountain ridges and the path of intuition and salmon runs and great literature and world Wisdom traditions and abiding friendships and the incessant following of the sweet scent of love? My mother and grandma were a bit doctrinaire, upon a time. But they weren't murderers or drug addicts. They loved the hell out of me, and taught by example even when the theological going got a bit rough. And my mother remains one of my closest friends, and she has never answered an Altar Call in her life because, in her own words, "I'm already a Christian, and that preacher has no right to try and shame me!" And in her view the presidency of G. W. Bush is "one big Altar Call." And she recently published a beautiful letter in a newspaper in defense of a river. So who's converted who here? Thanks to both of these strong women and (big hint to the children of fundamentalists everywhere!) to my ability to ignore these strong women, I am now a Jesus-loving ex-Adventist non-Christian novelist living in a gorgeous place, doing work I love, surrounded by people I love, including those female fundamentalists.

In short: "Why no bitterness?" Because I'm one lucky bounder!

IMAGE: How close is Gus's story in *The River Why* to your own? Was there a crossing, a conversion of sorts, as there was for Gus? An awakening? And did it come by way of the river?

DJD: Gus makes fly rods and ties trout flies for a living, and reads Wisdom literature and stands in rivers to keep his head on straight. I make nonfiction and fiction for a living, and read Wisdom literature and stand in rivers to keep my head on straight.

Was there a crossing? Yes. Did it come by way of the river? No. It came to me in every aspect of life—and so came to include rivers. Am I willing to talk about it? In my work, yes. But in an interview, hmmm. . . . Not directly. Some examples of what strikes me as "spirituality," as depicted in my work: Bill Bob's experience of "the Garden World" and Garden Angels in *The River Why*. Gus's experience of divine love at the climax of the same book. My own resolution of "the Mickey Mantle koan" in *River Teeth*. Kincaid Chance's vision of his father's impending death in the chapter called "Broken Boat" in *The Brothers K*. Everett Chance's experience of his dead father's presence in the story "Just Wind and a Creek" in *River Teeth*. Fly-fishing with Khwaja Khadir in *My Story as Told by Water*. Two essays in which I come out of the experiential closet a little, one called "Birdwatching as a Blood Sport," another called "Assailed."

But I believe in and love that closet. And that "Father who sees in secret" in there.

IMAGE: Denise Levertov writes about "work that enfaiths," meaning that the very process of engaging poetically with the story of Doubting Thomas (in her case) led her across the invisible border that divides that agnostic from the believer. I'm wondering if you've experienced anything similar to this. Was there, for instance, a piece of writing (your own or someone else's) that was absolutely crucial for you as an adolescent or in your twenties?

DJD: My writing work has not enfaithed me, in the sense that Levertov is talking about, though it strengthens the faith I already had by allowing me to lose my self (and so perhaps save it) for the better part of each day. What enfaithed me, though, was hollowing out, after years of effort, a little place in my heart about the size of a thimble. Then when I was twenty, in India one day, I turned to my best notion of God with embarrassed but complete sincerity, and said, "Would You care to fill this little thimble with anything?" And instantaneously—almost inanely, really—an undeniable, unimaginable, indescribable LAKE of peace and love landed on my head in reply.

But there's a "crossing story" for you. See what I mean about such stories being impossible to tell? "Duncan went to India and offered God a thimble to fill and instead a lake landed on his head. Great. That sounds like it will work for me, too. Anybody care to lend me a thimble and a plane ticket to India?" I was talking to Peter Matthiessen a few years back about spiritual experience—and we agreed that, while we each implicitly trust and are guided by our own such experiences, we almost completely distrust the other guy's. And isn't that the way it should be? It's fun to compare notes now and then. But the soul waiting to be uncovered—the soul waiting to save us while we keep burying it in dirty ego-juice—is our *own*, not someone else's. The fish I catch feed my family and me. The fish *you* catch, no offense, are just "fish stories" to me.

Now where were we?

IMAGE: I asked about writing experiences, or writings, that you've found transformative. If not writing by you, then by others?

DJD: Oh yeah. Thanks. Writings by others? There have been many. I've told, elsewhere, the story of how I got my sense of vocation from reading Thomas Mann's novel *Buddenbrooks* when I was sixteen and grief-stricken by the loss of a brother. It's too long and nuanced a story to conjure here, but I will say this. The teen years are often dark. When they are, it is dark literature and art that helps many of us begin to make sense of things. Dostoevsky, Shakespeare, *The Iliad*, *War and Peace*, Poe.

Once dark literature hooked me, though, I had an intravenous connection to an art form through which light began to flow. Hesse and Kazantzakis and Snyder and Kerouac were next. Then I leapt toward the primary Wisdom sources of which they spoke: Christian mysticism through Kazantzakis's St. Francis, Buddhism through the Beats, Vedanta through Hesse. I'm a lifelong reader of the *Gita* and *Tao te Ching*, and have lately become keen on the *Upanishads*. William Buck's novelization of the *Ramayana* is a masterpiece of Indian-spirituality-meets-American-lit. And I'm leaving out the books I feed upon most intensely because, as C. S. Lewis said, we can't always be defending our faith sources: it's more important to just feed on them. As Tukaram put it, *"Sing not the acts of Rama to hearts in whom love for Rama plays no part."*

Since you seem to be consumed by spiritual questions, though, Doug, I could offer to tell you—free of charge!—a story I've never told about how a crucial piece of writing affected me when I was about the age of your students here at Seattle Pacific . . .

IMAGE: Fire away.

DJD: I was a college sophomore, working graveyard shift as a janitor in order to study literature at Portland State University, when I bought a used copy of Meister Eckhart's sermons in a so-so Raymond Blakney translation. It's crucial to add that I picked the book up not for a class, but because I loved the first few words I read in it.

To paint my situation more fully: I'd been formally disinherited by my Adventist/Capitalist grandparents, for having left both their church and the fight for capital, in order to pursue my love of nature and of literature. I was unsupported by my parents, who'd just divorced and never had money anyway. I was too wild in high school to earn As and win scholarships. One of the last times I smoked pot was right before taking my SATs. My hope was to make myself useless to the Military-Industrial Complex. It worked—but made me useless to myself and everyone else. So I made myself useless to the Pot Complex as well. (Hippies were tragically slow to make this connection.)

On the recommendation of a teacher who recognized my self-sabotage for what it was, I made it into the Scholar's Program at Portland State University. But I was soon repelled by the critical, anti-intuitive, boxed-in academic thinking that I began to study and to emulate there. My heart's desire was to go to India on a pilgrimage, then move to a Northwest riverbank somewhere, work a blue-collar job, and start trying, on the side, to write a novel. If I left college, though, I was eligible for the draft and the Vietnam War. Better a mind box than a body bag, I figured. So I kept struggling along at school.

I was broke all the time in college—and I mean graceless, unpoignant, bald tires/bad food/bad house/bad teeth/bad breath broke. So one day I went to the food stamp office, and there learned that I qualified for the maximum student dole. To collect this dole, however, I had to sit for hours each month in the dank, dark, bureaucratic moat that surrounds all governmental giving.

While waiting in the food stamp office one day, I happened to open my new used Eckhart book to a sermon titled "God Laughs and Plays." I don't recall what scripture the Meister quoted in defense of this truth. And I refuse to look it up. There's too much dead text and too little living intuition in American spirituality these days! "God Laughs and Plays . . ." The title alone hooked me. I'd read enough Eckhart to know he was wiser than any Christian I'd met, and far wiser than me. I'd read enough to feel the glowering Republican "God" of fundamentalism losing his last shreds of power over me in the face of the unfathomable, loving mystery that is Eckhart's "unknown God." I'd read enough to know I trusted this sage with my mind and heart. And there in the food stamp office, the man I'd come to trust informed me that "God laughs and plays."

In disbelief, I began to cross-examine my hero. "He laughs?" I whispered.

Truly! Truly! insisted the Meister.

"He plays?" I asked.

The joy of all saints and angels together, answered Eckhart, *amounts to as little as a bean when compared to the joy of God at play.*

Why did I believe these crazy words? I don't know. Why did my life began to morph because of these words? I don't know. Given the grim death of my brother, the threat of the draft, threat of the war, plus my lifelong religious skepticism, the idea of a God who laughed and played seems incredibly unlikely to have pierced me. Yet the instant Eckhart declared it, things started to change.

The food stamp office, for instance. How ridiculous it began to look! So self-important. So institutional. So deliberately depressing. The monolithic metal desks and big swivel chairs of the bureacrats who bestowed the governmental largesse—as opposed to the dirty little molded plastic chairs for us rabble. The brain-bending tubelights' "liberty and justice for all." The place seemed conspiratorially designed by some Nazi Martha Stewart out to create oceans of ambient guilt in poor people.

The rules, too, began to seem ridiculous. That the ailing, half-wrecked, unhirable folks who dragged themselves in here had to lie every visit, as I did, saying that we'd been out hunting jobs, in order to collect our stamps! Not only did it make us feel guilty, it taught us that lying is necessary in order to survive.

In short: the place suddenly struck me as so concertedly Kafkaesque, and the news that God laughs and plays was so explosively non-Kafka, that I began to grin at the whole clumsily officious arrangement. How could I take the food stamp procedure seriously when, somewhere above or inside every grim molecule of it, God was laughing and playing so joyously that the joy of all the saints and angels didn't amount to a bean in comparison?

As soon as I started to think this, I too started to feel joy. And in its presence, I found I could no longer do what I was doing. The grubby plastic chair beneath my ass suddenly struck me as hilarious. Then so did the buzz of the tubelights, the guilt-inducing rules, the shame-inducing stamps. Then so did my fear of going to Vietnam. If God laughed and played, I could laughingly refuse to serve in 'Nam! If God laughed and played, it was ridiculous of me to be eking out an American half-life according to so many tiny-minded, miserable little rules. I stood up. I snapped Eckhart's sermons shut. "God laughs and plays," I told the food stamp office, "and I'm outta here!" And I never went back again.

That's a crazy-sounding story, I realize, and it leaves what we tend to call "reality" out. So let me say how I dealt, in nuts and bolts, with my loss of governmental nutrition assistance.

I kept reading Eckhart, for starters, and fell ever deeper in love with what he, and Jesus before him, and Buddha before Him, refer to by various names as "spiritual poverty." Contemplating this mysterious condition, I aspired to master an American rendition of it. I ate less, or ate cheaper. More important, I wanted less. Wanted next to nothing. And learned that desires aren't wants—learned, when I felt restless, felt like shopping, felt like being coddled or entertained, to say *I don't want!* and be happy. I found a warehouse that sold dented cans of Campbell's soups, Van Camp's pork and beans, Western Family apricots, and bought them by the case. When the cans didn't explode at the insertion of the can opener, I ate the contents. When they did explode, I ducked and thought: *God laughs and plays.* I picked pounds of every fruit in season, rented a dump of a house with a beautiful garden space, learned to garden, harvest, and store, ate three-day-old bakery goods I bought for next to nothing, snuck off to my beloved rivers, caught trout, salmon, steelhead, whitefish, bluegill, bass, commended them to their laughing playing Creator, clobbered them, cooked them, thanked them, and ate them.

It wasn't an easy life. No novacaine at the dentist. No health (or at times even car) insurance. Little travel, no restaurants, few movies. But lots and lots of what George McDonald calls "sacred leisure." Staying alert to opportunities both spiritual and material, but giving the spiritual the ruling hand, I worked hard, lived with the "discretionary funding" of the average American dog, invoked a laughing playing God, and achieved a pretty darn dignified poverty-line existence. I lived on six grand a year for the ten or so years it took me to get started as a writer, actually. And I believe even today, summer 2001, that though six grand wouldn't cut it, the so-called poverty line would. I believe people might amaze themselves with their ingenuity, energy, creativity, and modesty of need if their modus operandi became a deep conviction that God laughs and plays.

13

• • • • • • • •

The Only Son

part of a letter to my friend Deb Blue,
a Christian preacher

... I don't know much, but it seems to me that the crucifixion took place in eternity, which is another way of saying
"takes place forever," which is another way of saying "takes
place now." It seems to me that my ignorance is his suffering,
this and every instant, and that Jesus is even more human
than I am (not less!), and that his suffering is vivid and real
and agonizing. It seems to me that this word you and all
good Christians love, "salvation," emanates from an ongoing
salvific act (not just an historic one) just as the sunbeams
that create and sustain life here on earth emanate from a
still-shining, still-conflagrating, still-self-sacrificing sun.
It seems to me you know all that. And call it "The Cross."
But for some reason you don't seem to know that so is
"Enlightenment" a word that emanates, sunlike, from an
endlessly shining salvific act: the Bo Tree Act. And no one
(especially not a Minnesotan or Montanan!) could possibly
begin to respect or adore that Act unless they studied it in
some detail, fought their way in past the superficial foreign-
ness of it, heard some of the heart music in it, and chose
to imbibe the story as something more than an Oriental

curiosity, snorted line of spiritual cocaine, or cause for fantasized jealousy between Buddhists and Christians. Until we sit down and realize that we too are stuck, this and every instant, at the foot of the same Tree, the Bo Tree Act is, so to speak, just a bad Bertolucci movie starring Keanu Reaves as Buddha.

In short: I'm damned glad you're standing strong in the sunbeam named Christianity. But the existence of your beam does nothing to lessen the intensity or reality of the other beams. If you don't have time to move over and stand in the radiance of any others, that's fine, that's great, you've got yours and One's plenty. I just happen to have glimpsed a couple of others—which is the reason I talk about them.

You say, "I want to believe Christ and Buddha and God and the Tao and Grace and the Bo Tree and the Cross are the same because it makes it all seem bigger and better and more likely to be true . . ." I can't put it in quite that way. In all honesty, I have to say that, by the light of inner experience (supplemented by years of study, and years of friendship with other lovers of the same truth), the Bo Tree and the Cross are the same. I don't "want to believe this." I can't begin not to. Nothing comes to me when I try. (I guess I never was a very good fundy, though I was raised by some of the best!)

Shakyamuni's determination to find salvific truth was Absolute. It was "The Crucifixion of the Son." He refused to run. He nailed himself in place. He fasted so long, it is said, that the bones of his spinal column could be felt through his abdomen from the front side!

But ah, words. We need a film by Mel Gibson to do this self-sacrifice visual justice.

Speaking of visuals: those curlicues covering the head of the myriad Buddha statues? Do you know what I heard

those depict? Sit down some day in August heat on the
south side of a tree and stay there a while without water,
without moving, like the prince Gautama. Pretend you, like
he, have commited to an insanely irreversible vow to save
all sentient beings from suffering and death or die trying.
When your brain starts to fry, which will be soon, meditate
on the fact that this young, beautiful, heretofore happily
married father sat just like you're sitting, day in and day
out, night in and night out, with no option but this:

†

Truth or death.

Those curlicues? Snails, I've been told, that crawled up onto
the coming Buddha's head, knowing he'd never make it, he'd
die without them. Snails from Earth herself and Water
herself, miraculously moved by a mortal man's yearning to
achieve Truth for the sake of all sentient beings including
snails, or die trying. Think about a snail. They're so barely
sentient it's as if Earth and Water themselves were reaching
up to cover the would-be savior's head, Earth and Water
saying to him, *"What are you doing, sweet man! This sun/Son
stuff's gonna kill ya! Stop, why don't you? Are you listening to
us? No? Okay then. Let us help!"* The impending Shakyamuni
not caring one way or the other. Not altering his set course,
even to acknowledge this act of supreme tenderness. And
why?

Because he can't. He's nailed to a Tree.

And then—(when you figure out precisely how this
works, Deb, tell me!)—he's Free.

Tree, roots, trunk, branches, earth, sky, universe, snails,
End, Beginning, Majesty.

No more lowercase "h" now. No one seated there but
He.

So see how slight the difference between us? And feel how little it matters?

St. Francis said to God, "No one is worthy to pronounce Thy Name." So Buddhists don't. You hope the Bo and Cross are one. And I can only hear Truth being told when Buddhist Enlightenment is Christian Son of Godhood. Nothing in me can any longer keep them separate. Enlightenment is the man Gautama or Jesus, dead, and the Christ/Buddha rising from the base of the Bo or waking from three days behind the Rock. That's the famous part of the stories. And a less famous part I dearly love:

It can't have gone well for those curlicues on Shakya-muni's sunbaked head. So, so is the Cross the snails' sweet sacrifice for the all-sacrificing Son. Those curlicues are a field of cool wet Crosses, field of Bos, on the Lord's very head.

Think of the distance, in terms of consciousness, from snailhood to Godhood! Isn't there room, on this vast span, for your Rock-of-Ages-type grandparents and mine, and for the tiny bit of difference between us?

14

◆ ◆ ◆ ◆ ◆ ◆ ◆

Nonfiction
vs.
Fiction
vs.
Cosmic Illusion

There is an old, broken ponderosa pine tree, backlit by evening sunlight, outside the window as I write these words. This tree is real. It is "nonfiction." But the words "pine tree, backlit by evening sunlight" are neither the tree nor the light: they are signals telling the imagination to create an imaginary tree and light. The difference between actual tree and signal tree is the reason I prefer the way it feels to write fiction to the way it feels to write so-called nonfiction. Fiction writing feels more honest to me. The whole notion of so-called nonfiction—of a form of writing that does not involve making the tree, the light, and everything else, up— strikes me as, well, a fiction. The aims of fact-based writing are as noble as those of fiction writing. But to write a prose that goes by the name "nonfiction" is to be tempted to forget that one is writing imaginatively, like everyone else, while refusing to admit it.

We see into our memories in much the way we see across the floor of a sunbaked desert: everything we imaginatively conjure—every object, creature, or event we perceive "back there"—is distorted, before it reaches us, by mirages created by subjectivity, time, and distance. Fiction writers are fairly comfortable with these distortions, because fiction is itself a controlled series of mirages. Nonfiction writers, in their claim to be presenting "reality," are less comfortable—sometimes so much less comfortable that they deny the existence of any distortion in their prose. Such denials are nonsense. To say of any past event "I remember exactly what happened" is an exaggeration so great we might as well call it false. Even first-hand perception is an imperfect medium. Witness our sun and moon, seemingly equal in size, perceptibly orbiting a flat Earth. Memory's transmissions are also imperfect, and personal desire spins the imperfection further. Compare, for example, any Utah Indian tribe's mythological history of their homeland to a triumphalist Mormon history of the same terrain. Nonfiction meets nonfiction. And no agreement whatsoever.

This is why I feel that the best a would-be nonfiction writer can do is use imperfect language to invoke imperfectly remembered events based on imperfect perceptions. The best that any of us can do, in other words, is tell a story.

There is a superstition—fed most savagely these days by the news media—holding that what we hear firsthand is "true" or "real" and that what we merely imagine is "untrue" or "unreal." News reports on what the president babbled about Iraq or Iran today, for instance, are real, while the works of Dickens, Twain, and Dostoevsky are not. This is nonsense. Insofar as literature enlivens imaginations, firms our grasp of reality, or strengthens our regard for fellow humans, it serves the world. And insofar as the president speaks scripts that deny life-threatening facts or erode the careful distinctions that sustain civil discourse and international goodwill, the "real" news report merely disseminates propaganda. Reportage can, and daily does, lie. Even firsthand experience can lie. And "mere" imaginary experience can open us to truths that would remain inaccessible forever if we had to wait for reportage or experience to teach us the same truth.

The popularity—particularly in film and television, but in weak nonfiction, too—of paltry narratives calculated to appeal to an audience because they are "based on a true story" implies a dangerous forgetfulness of the fact that even "true stories" are imaginative reconstructions teeming with the deletions, distortions, and prejudices of their creators. The false testimony of every guilty party ever tried in a court of law is "based on a true story"—a true story ever-so-slightly spun, in hopes of avoiding punishment, into truth-bending lies. Mass media, with its "true story" bias, routinely pretends that such truth-bending does not exist.

Even when our intentions are the opposite of criminal, no facsimile is the same as its original: to remember anything whatsoever, then write of or film it, is to create a work not "of reality" but of the human imagination. To write of or to film things is to arrange, rearrange, impose emphases, assign order, and render an artful incompleteness upon things. Each frame of a film or sentence of a narrative represents an act of imaginative selection on the part of an author, a director, a cinematographer. In this sense even the most straight-faced PBS documentaries or exacting science texts are a form of fiction writing—and to refuse to acknowledge this fact forces the terms "nonfiction" and "true story" to make promises they're woefully unable to keep.

There are differences in any two writers' degree of reliance upon facts, and differences of purpose in their manipulation of them. But the "facts" can easily be arranged to conceal, obfuscate, exaggerate or negate the truth. Think of the environmental lawyers hired by corporations not to protect ecosystems but to compose fictions that help corporations create an illusion of ecological responsibility. Or of virtually any PR firm's fact spinners: the PR firm sells concealment, obfuscation, exaggeration, and negation to whoever can afford to purchase it, so they can pawn it off to the public as "truth."

Writers determined to purge all fiction from their nonfiction rebel against the gray zones I'm describing. Some even concoct alternative terms for fiction and nonfiction, which they claim are more precise: "event-based imaginative writing versus non-event-based imaginative writing," for example. But a lot of fiction is event-based, and a lot of nonfiction is pure imaginative speculation. Terminology is not the problem here: the problem is that the kind of imaginative writing called "nonfiction" is inextricably tangled in the kind of imaginative writing called "fiction," and vice versa, and those who want their categories to be "pure" may as well start wringing their hands.

The dictionary is helpful on this topic in that it's no help at all. My unabridged *Random House* defines fiction as "the class of literature comprising works of imaginative narration, especially in prose form." It defines nonfiction as "the branch of literature comprising works of narrative prose dealing with or offering opinions or conjectures upon facts and reality." One can almost smell the lexicographers' panic here. Seeing that their supposed opposites are virtually identical, they add an anxious parenthesis to the definition of nonfiction, calling it "opposed to fiction and distinguished from poetry and drama." But how is it opposed? To call nonfiction a "branch of literature" and fiction a "class of literature" is random word choice, not a valid distinction. And to call fiction "imaginative narration in prose form" and nonfiction "narrative prose" merely hides the troublesome word "imaginative" from the nonfiction admirer's field of vision. Similarly, to say that nonfiction writers "offer opinions or conjectures upon facts or reality" does not alter the fact that fiction writers do the same.

Admirers of nailed-down definitions and "pure" categories may not want to hear it, but all writers and readers are full-time imaginers, all prose is imaginative, and fiction and nonfiction are two incestuously related shades of ink swirling in the same mysterious well. Those of us who would tell a story can only dip in our quills and start writing. To claim full certainty as to which shade of ink we're using is to claim to have achieved a perfection toward which we mortals, with our swirly ink and swirlier imaginations and memories, can only aspire.

In support of this conclusion I'd like to offer—in the manner of such "nonfiction" publications as textbooks and popular magazines—a pop quiz.

Label the following ten paragraphs Fiction or Nonfiction:

1) The sun has now set behind the ponderosa out my window, but is still shining on the ponderosa on my essay's first page. [Fiction:__ Nonfiction:__]

2) For some time now the evening news has been drifting in from the living room. Out in California (I hear Tom Brokaw reporting from New York), the Sierra Club has filed suit

against Walt Disney Enterprises for engraving the head of Mickey Mouse into the side of the world's tallest living redwood, though Disney had legally purchased the land upon which the tree stands. [Fiction:__ Nonfiction:__]

3) I remember reading, back in the '70s, that almost every cell in our bodies dies and is replaced by a fresh cell within seven years. This means that if we've been married for seven years and still have sex with our spouse we are guilty of infidelity, for we no longer make love to the body we wed. It also means that if we remember anything from further back than seven years—including this statement about the lifespan of cells—we remember it with different cells than the ones that recorded the memory, hence it is not the same memory, hence we don't remember it at all. [Fiction:__ Nonfiction:__]

4) The unfaithful cells of our bodies are a microcosmic reminder that Earth herself is just a finite number of sub-stances endlessly reconstituting themselves—via the pro-cesses we call birth, death, growth, and decay—into an endless variety of forms. "The general cosmic dissolution" was Lord Krishna's term for this. "Night falls, and all are dis-solved into the sleeping germ of life," Krishna told Arjuna, anticipating our "New Physics" by some three thousand years. "Dissolving with the dark, and with day returning back to new birth, new death: all helpless; all doing what they must." My own helpless body, even without dying, has already reconstituted itself so many times on the energetic and cellular levels that to call it "my body" is a kind of lie. We all consist, literally, of unownable matter and energy. We consist, nonfictively, of each other and of ancient dust—of ancient ashes, fire, air, and water; ancient bone, blood, shit, and clay. [Fiction:__ Nonfiction:__]

5) American Indians knew their New Physics. The wisest among them intuitively knew—and lived and worshipped in ways that proved they knew—that all creatures are being constantly molded, kiln-fired, broken, ground to dust, re-molded and refired into all other creatures. This is one reason why they didn't bother to kill on the spot the seventeenth-century Dutch shmuck who believed he'd hoodwinked their homeland away from them. Peter Minuit. That was his name, wasn't it? And how pitiably bizarre he must have seemed to the constantly dead and reborn, unmade and re-made Indians to whom he offered a pile of perfectly good nails and fishhooks in exchange for the right to pretend that the constantly dying and resurrecting isle of bone, blood, shit, and clay now called "Manhattan" had become the "per-manent possession" of his constantly deconstituting recon-stituting self. [Fiction:__ Nonfiction:__]

6) Of course Minuit believed he'd scored the deal of all time. He gloated over his fishhooks-for-Manhattan trade all the way to his grave. He then rotted in that grave, be-came soil and worms in an old Dutch cemetery, became a dumptruckload of dirt in a subway excavation, became fill for a housing tract in Jersey, a backyard vegetable garden, scarlet runner beans, corn, and compost, became an evening meal, a bowel movement, a little energy and thought, a byte of Americana, then maybe some small karma-balancing ac-tion (a lost twenty-dollar bill, an IRS fine, a bank error in our disfavor) in the lives of you and me. Four hundred rent-controlled apartments now tower over the spot where the Indians made off with their useful fishhooks. Not one of them houses a Minuit. [Fiction:__ Nonfiction:__]

7) Fiction is nonfiction and nonfiction fiction because this is a world in which nothing remains distinct from anything

else for long. Light is a form of energy, matter a form of energy, and both are in a state of constant flux—a state of No Real State—even as we observe them in fictitious stasis. Minuit's and all Manhattan's cells and memories are, therefore, our own, and "our own" will soon be someone else's. Krishna's three-thousand-year-old Law of General Cosmic Dissolution is, in short, our physical reality. But, again according to Krishna, there is stupendous cause for this fact: the reason that nothing on this earth remains distinct from anything else for long, the reason no Brokaw, Minuit, Mickey Mouse, or Duncan can possess anything for long, is that this is a world in which we're eventually bound to possess everything. "Behind the manifest and unmanifest there is an Existence that is eternal and changeless," says Krishna, opening a door in the wall of physics to reveal what Christ called kingdom. "This Existence is not dissolved in the general cosmic dissolution. Fools pass blindly by it, and of its majesty know nothing. It is nearer than knowing. I am that Existence, O son of Kunti. I am that place of refuge. I am the breaking apart, the dissolution, the end of the path, the beginning, the changeless, the place of abode. I lie under the seen. And they that love me shall not perish." [Fiction:__ Nonfiction:__]

8) "Give everything to the poor and follow me," another transphysicist, Jesus of Nazareth, once recommended. "The very idea!" huffed the avowed Christian, Minuit, only to become a vegetable garden then an IRS fine. But seven hundred years after Krishna and five hundred before Christ, Gautama, crown prince of the Shakyas, did indeed give everything to the poor, wandered off into Indian wilderness, sat down beneath a wild Bo tree, remained there as if nailed to it hand and foot, and eventually realized that in this perfect poverty he possessed everything—tree, wilder-

ness, majesty, end of path, place of abode, and all that he'd given away. [Fiction:__ Nonfiction:__]

9) In light of contemporary banking or real estate or tax-form logic, we must agree with Peter Minuit that Christ's recommendation to give all to the poor is a nondeductible recipe for self-inflicted penury and all the misery that goes with it. In light of Krishna's Law of General Cosmic Dissolution, however, Christ's words become a physics-loving, truth-telling admission of our long-term economic and bodily state. In the end we possess nothing: not our homes, not our cells, not our memories, not our physical remains. In other words, in the end we possess only fiction. So in giving all we own—be it Manhattan, or these sentences—to the poor, we give away fiction. [Fiction:__ Nonfiction:__]

10) All human giving is fiction giving. Only the Absolute nonfictively owns; hence only the Absolute can nonfictively give; hence the mortal who believes that he or she owns, stands no chance of receiving what the Absolute has to nonfictively give. Christ's recommendation to give away everything is not a recipe for bankruptcy. It is an invitation to partake, like Shakyamuni beneath the Bo tree, in an invincibly nonfictive state. In this world of illusion, flux, and euphemism, we call this nonfictive state "poverty." But this poverty is the sweet nakedness that lies beneath the seen. And we need only grasp it to enter it. To know that we can possess nothing, and live accordingly, is to have given away everything, and so to have become the very poor to whom the Absolute is forever giving. [Fiction:__ Nonfiction:__]

There is an old pine tree, pierced by the light of stars, outside the window as I write these words. We call such trees

"Ponderosas." But what did the humans here call them throughout the unknowable flow of seasons before botany became Botany, America became America, and English became English?

As the proud owner, in the long run, of nothing but fiction, all I can say for certain is that the tree out my window is, like me, a temporary alliance of shared energies and memories, ancient friends, loves and enemies, ancient blood, shit, and clay. All I can say is that, under the slow, seen dissolution, I sense the Prince of the Shakyas still seated at its base, Jesus still nailed to its trunk, and Krishna still perched in its branches, the clear notes of fiction flying from his flute. All I can say is that, though I am typing even the words "nakedness," "love," and "poverty" into a silicon medium I neither love nor understand; and though I read, like anyone, the "true" and terrible news stories; though I hear the log trucks, jets, and gunshots in the actual and televised distances and fear our 6.5 billion appetites, vanishing salmon and native grasses, vanishing frogs, forests, sperm counts, vanishing graces, races, tongues, I keep watching that tree—base, trunk, and branches: its certain end; certain beginning; endless majesty.

I keep watching, day and night. And listening to, and for, His notes.

Assailed

improvisations in the key of cosmology

> *Each living creature (is) . . . a little universe, formed of*
> *a host of self-propagating organisms, inconceivably*
> *minute and as numerous as the stars in heaven.*
>
> CHARLES DARWIN

> *For every Space larger than a red Globule of Man's blood*
> *is visionary . . . And every Space smaller than a*
> *Globule of Man's blood opens into Eternity of*
> *which this vegetable Earth is but a shadow.*
>
> WILLIAM BLAKE

JOURNAL ENTRY

The countless things that fit in our minds and imaginations
do so because they are abstract. Abstraction, in this sense, is
wonderfully useful: it is what makes memories and knowledge
portable, art, science, and stories possible, and music, images
and experiences had or heard by a "you" capable of moving
through time and space into a "me."

The danger of abstraction is that the matter and life-forms
that surround and sustain us are not abstract. Our actions

unleash forces latent in abstract concepts upon matter and living forms. These concepts, if insufficiently faithful to life, cause harm.

When the universe speaks to us, it does not use words. We are all involved, daily, in translating Creation's nonverbal messages into abstract thought and language. To live in harmony with other life-forms and one another, our translations must be accurate. If, for instance, we flaunt meteorologists and wear shorts and a t-shirt at ten below, we freeze; if we defy soil scientists and irrigate with alkaline water, our gardens wither; if we flaunt the EPA, power our cities with coal-fired electricity, and fill the air, soil, and foods with mercury, thousands suffer and die.

This is why we require cosmologies. Cosmology is Creation and abstraction engaged in imaginative negotiation. It is mind, matter, and spirit at play. Stories too literally rooted in tradition can lose this living playfulness. In Leviticus 14, for example, Moses urges the priests of his day to end outbreaks of epidemic disease by catching two birds, killing one of them, and washing the infected person's house with both the living bird's body and the dead bird's blood. To worship such a scripture by literalizing it dishonors the scripture's life-giving intent, dooms the diseased, and needlessly kills birds.

Moses was a living, breathing, spontaneous, and capable man, not an archaic list of dos and don'ts: his cosmology was a series of creative responses to ever-changing circumstances. And for all his wisdom, Moses had a famously short fuse. Were such a man living here and now, trying to honor his Creator as he learned, say, that human-caused global warming could melt the 450 billion metric tons of carbon stored in permafrost, setting off a "carbon bomb" that could make Earth uninhabitable to countless life-forms including Moses' people, it's hard for me to believe that coal-fired power plants, gas-hog vehicles, and single-car commutes wouldn't become the "abominations" that called forth his famed "thou-shalt-nots."

A cosmological story, though built of abstract language, must accurately translate the here and now. Though informed by scripture and tradition, such stories should inhale what's fresh and exhale what's stale; should cross-pollinate and migrate if needed, morph if needed, reason, intuit, imagine, and respond as needed. The best cosmological speculation, it therefore seems, might unfold in a manner more like an improvised raga or jazz tune than a classical recital. A jazz pianist or sitar player can, on a given occasion, pull trained instincts from his fingers and structures from his mind, interact with keyboard or fretboard, and extemporaneously produce music unique to place and time. Shouldn't the possessor of a viable cosmology be able to do the same?

I live in the extreme upper Columbia River system, in the Bitterroot Mountains' rain shadow, in a cottonwood and willow creek-bottom between 7,000-foot ridges. We call the year 2005, the season spring. Can I extemporaneously pull trained instincts from my fingers and structures from my mind to produce a series of cosmological improvisations in response to this place and time?

Assignment: find out. Sit down and see whether you can improvise, jazz- or raga-style, a series of cosmological riffs based on what is materially and spiritually perceptible here and now; what is moving through time and space with you; what you see, hear, feel, dream, and intuit, this day and always, to be true. . . .

IMPROVISATION #1: STARS, CELLS, SNOW

It is March in Montana and the door between winter and spring is swinging violently. For days a sometimes-gentle, sometimes-brutal southwesterly wind has been breaking over the Bitterroot Mountains, bringing walls of cloud so vast and near-black they look world-ending. Each dark wall dumps a load of snow. An impossibly blue sky then breaks out. The snow grows blinding, melts, birds burst into arias, summer feels just round the corner. But then, tied to the balm like an anti-proverbial March lion to its lamb, the next cloud wall appears, hurtling the world back an entire season.

Studying this weather as I drive my daughters to school, I return home, go to my desk to work, look round the room, and realize that after a winter of writing my study looks as if the same weather has been blasting through it. Setting aside the manuscript I'd planned to work on, I fetch a dust-cloth and cardboard box and set out to restore order. An hour into this work I start to recycle two old magazines (a *Time* and a *National Geographic*), but first open the *Time* to save a grouse-feather "bookmark." The page the feather was marking stops me in my tracks:

It's a Hubble Space Telescope photo of clouds in the Orion Nebula. They're 1,500 light-years (roughly 10,000,000,000, 000,000,000 miles) from Montana and me. They're made not of ice crystals, like the clouds outside, but of superheated hydrogen that lights them from within. In color they range from orange to gold to rosewood brown, pierced here and there by tiny flares of bright pink. In form they're flagrantly phallic, and remind me of stalagmites, velvet moose antlers, coral formations, basalt columns on the lower Columbia River and, begging our pardon, one of the exceedingly odd parts of Everyman. In size, though, the Orion clouds annihilate all earthly analogy: they are six trillion miles long.

There are projections coming off them. Shaped like animal ears, bean sprouts, the antennae of slugs (some artfully tipped by the pink flares), the protuberances are tiny compared to the masses out of which they grow. Yet even the smallest, the Hubble astronomers tell us, are as wide as our entire solar system. And even the smallest contain something astounding:

stars.

Those piercingly pink flares? They're foetal stars, every one of them, caught by the Hubble camera in the very process of being born. What's more, the astronomers tell us, our sun, solar system, Earth, its hydrogen, oxygen, water, life-forms, you, me, are all the offspring of these same type of clouds.

For the first time it hits me: the sun, Earth, and I are siblings. Despite our obvious vast differences, we're each the progeny of just such stupendous clouds. As I sit by my Montana window I am seated in the light of an Ancient Brother, on the lap of an Ancient Sister, looking, as if in a family album, at a photo of three Heavenly Father/ Mothers. This gives me a feeling so paradoxical it makes me dizzy. I am so tiny and short-lived compared to the Orion parent-clouds! Yet I share a progenitive shape with them, I've conceived offspring as have they, and my offspring shine like stars to me.

A wondrous fact from a book I've been reading (Sara Maitland's *A Joyful Theology*): the number of cells in the human body is almost exactly the same as the number of stars in the Milky Way. Is this meaningless coincidence or a purposeful symmetry devised by our Creator? I have no idea. I only know that some facts make me happy, and that a flurry of such facts have begun to whirl through me now.

Fact: the spring day has darkened and snow is swirling and falling again.

Fact: a contradictorily bright feeling is sweeping through me.

Fact: I am sitting amid mountains, pondering a celestial cloud whose "snow" is stars and a terrestrial cloud whose "stars" are snow; my children and I each have a Milky Way's worth of cells burning in our bodies; and our galaxy has a human being's worth of star-cells shining in its vast swirl.

IMPROVISATION #2: TRUE WILDERNESS

Recalling now why I saved the dusty *National Geographic*, I open it, and am sure enough struck dumb by a Hubble Space photo even grander than that of the Orion Nebula.

To capture this image the telescope was aimed, as the astronomers describe it, at one of the darkest parts of space, focused on an interstellar region "the size of a grain of sand held at arms's length," and 276 exposures were taken over ten days "to gather as much distant light as possible." The result is a photograph not of layers of stars, but of layers of *galaxies*, literally thousands of them in this single image, stretching "as far as the Hubble's eye can see."

I walk slowly back through this. Here's a mere speck of our universe, a sand-sized grain of it, yet when a 276-exposure jury turns in its verdict, the grain is seen to contain a vast field of jeweled galaxies glittering in blankness and blackness. The physical gaze of this photo has penetrated so deep it's become spiritual. It tells a story too vast for thought or word, yet here it sits on a page, speaking a beyond-language of spheres, swirls, colors, light. Even the tiniest points in this image, the astronomers say, are not stars but entire galaxies. The light from some, traveling at 186,000 miles per second, takes eleven billion years to reach Earth.

This is what I call a Roadless Area! This is true Wilderness. The number of stars, star-birthing nebula-clouds, solar systems, planets, moons, mineral-forms, life-forms, dead-forms, implied by this single photo stops my mind and leaves me hearing music. If we could look back toward ourselves from some bright point herein depicted, the entire Milky Way would be a shining dot, our sun a nothingness lost in that dot, our Earth and selves a dream within nothingness.

What also strikes me, what consoles and soothes me here, is the realization that Earth is at one not with humanity, but with this fathomless multi-galaxied swirl. Lacking some sci-fi miracle such as "warp speed" that lets us travel millions of times faster than light, not a molecule of this vastness shall ever be disturbed, colonized, debated, exploited, degraded, or even touched by our curiously manipulative species. Human folly has knocked some of our own natural systems out of balance, and has created extinctions that throw the evolution of forms backward in time. But the birthing of stars, cooling of stars into planets, creation and evolution of planetary life, are inexorable. Earth will swirl on. It's only a speck of a species known as "terrestrial humanity" that may not. The wilderness in this photograph contains us the way a shoreless ocean contains a drop. Even at our grandiose worst, we are a negligible jot of darkness in a boundlessness filled with symmetries, mysteries, and lights.

IMPROVISATION #3: ASSAILED

On a five-foot shelf within reach of my desk I keep forty or so books I've read so often that their imaginative flights and insights now bleed into my own. Turning from the Hubble photos to this shelf, my eyes alight on Annie Dillard's *For the Time Being*. Why? I seem to remember words spoken by Annie's hero, the French paleontologist, priest, and mystic, Teilhard de Chardin, that once left me feeling the same silent music as these spring snow clouds and Hubble images.

I page through the book till the inner music and Teilhard's words mesh:

By means of all created things, without exception, the divine assails us, penetrates us, and molds us. We imagined it as distant and inaccessible, whereas in fact we live steeped in its burning layers.

These words somehow reverse the Hubble image, throwing the swirl of galaxies into my interior, then covering my body head to toe with goose bumps. It seems an unnecessary act of cosmic exhibitionism when, out the window, sunlight bursts forth, the finches, crossbills, grosbeaks, and siskins burst into song, and now-blinding snowflakes keep swirling down. Turning from snow to galaxies to embryonic pink stars to a desk photo of my daughters, I am assailed. My youngest, in the photo, holds a single petal of a living sunflower. The same flower's blind eye followed the sun across the sky every day last summer, then in autumn bowed low, and in winter fed its eye to the birds. The birds repaid it by planting bits of eye in the dirt. Tiny green sprouts now unfurl all over our yard. The sun is burning four million tons of itself per second to enliven this world of birds, sunflowers, and melting snow. Agéd suns explode like old blossoms, their fragments scattering, falling into orbits, becoming planets. The seeds of future suns gestate in fiery phallus clouds.

The sunlit snow is a falling Milky Way. The cells of my body are another. We are born of and fed by a sacrificial burning. We live steeped in its layers. My daughters' brown eyes burn so serenely—yet they burn. The music of Teilhard's words rises. Tears rise. I turn from stars to sunlight to sunflowers to snow to my children's faces. I feel us steeping in the sacrificial layers.

IMPROVISATION #4:
SCIENCE & REVERENCE

I consider the infinite wilds to be the divine manuscript. I hold these wilds to be the only unbowdlerized copy we have of the Book that gives and sustains life. Human industry is shredding this gift like an Enron document. There are those who call the shredding "free market economics" or just plain "freedom." It's not exactly a lie. But the freedom to shred the divine manuscript is not an economics any lover of neighbor, self, or earth wishes to practice. Once self-forgetfulness and self-giving start to give back joy, one grows bewildered by the worship of selfishness, chucks the politics of self-interest, and casts about for less ephemeral hopes.

A new source of hope for me: the growing reverence for nature and its mysteries among scientists. This reverence marks a significant development in consciousness: the sciences, until quite recently, were committed to mechanistic paradigms and an obsession with the physically measurable that made reverence possible only by disconnecting spirituality and scientific thought. The so-called Enlightenment and its empirical thinking led, sans spirit, to the effective naming of things, cataloguing of things, dissecting, extracting, and reconstruction of things, creating the modern world as we pretended, for a time, to know it. By the late twentieth century, the same divorce between spirituality and science had led to filing copyrights on ancient living things; to the genetic warping of living things; to raping, monoculturizing, and extirpating entire species of living things; and, ultimately, to abstracting ourselves from living things as if we were not living things ourselves.

I see two chief causes for the countering outburst of reverence in science, one famous, the other infamous.

The famous cause: the new physics. Quantum mechanics has changed the way we see the universe. The old proton/neutron/electron atom has become as unfit for describing matter as a typewriter is unfit for surfing the Web. Atomic particles are now believed to derive from immaterial wave packets; space is said to have had ten original dimensions that collapsed, at the beginning of time, to form the superstrings of which subatomic particles consist. Field theory; wave mechanics; morphogenesis; the recently discovered "tunneling" of electrons through neutrons. Through a multitude of images and equations, physics is now telling us that Space, Time, and Matter derive from a source infinitely subtler and greater than all three.

The infamous cause of the new reverence among scientists: suffering. How many biologists, botanists, ethnologists, anthropologists, have been forced to renounce their fields in mid-career because their living objects of study have died out before their eyes? How many more have been so dismayed by the world's barrios, biological dead or disease zones, slave labor and oil war zones, that they've abandoned their disciplines to become peace activists or humanitarians? I'm not going to belabor these ubiquitous problems, but I touch on them to introduce a sentence that strikes me as pivotal: humanity's serious problems, said Albert Einstein, "cannot be solved at the same level of consciousness that created them." What is most needed, if this deceptively simple statement is true, is not just problem solving, but change in the level of our consciousness.

That emininently practical man, E. F. Schumacher, appears to have agreed with Einstein. Though famed for his problem-solving masterpiece on appropriate technologies, *Small Is Beautiful*, Schumacher ended his career with *A Guide for the Perplexed*—a meticulous, metaphysical tour de force on human levels of consciousness and how to raise them. Teilhard de Chardin strikes me, in this context, as a person in whom humanity's problems have been largely solved—for any human whom the divine is "assailing, penetrating, and molding" is not living at a level of consciousness willing to shred the divine manuscript in the name of an abstract "freedom."

The lives of Einstein, Schumacher, and Teilhard make me wonder: what would happen if the world's would-be problem solvers focused less exclusively on the problems coming at them? Einstein and Teilhard were renowned for the absent-minded, walk-about states in which their greatest insights came to them. I sense more here than a quirk shared by two eccentric men.

What if our primary focus became the way in which we greeted the dawn, our every breath, our burning, and only then did we turn to face the problems?

IMPROVISATION #5: TOWARD LIVING LANGUAGE

The human brain is the most complex physical object in the known universe. Its ten billion neurons, says scientist Gerald Edelman, can make a million billion interconnections. Our thoughts and dreams fire lucidly or weave drunkenly through our cortexes in patterns as complex as stars gyring through a galaxy. Yet Sir John Carew Eccles, the Nobel Prize–winning brain researcher, tells us that the brain is not itself the cause or source of its own synaptic voltage. The brain doesn't produce energies: it only receives them. Picking up invisible impulses, it transposes them into data that the ego consciousness can translate. The energies themselves, says Eccles, come from a realm inaccessible to any known method of measurement—a realm we could easily call "spiritual."

We live in an era when scientific concepts are expanding so fast that the lexicon of science, if it is to reflect these changes, must expand as well. The direction the world's best minds keep suggesting we take this expansion is inward, to the realm of spirit.

The Benedictine contemplative Willigis Jager, in his book *Search for the Meaning of Life*, describes many convergences between the new physics and metaphysics. The microelectromagnetic forces known as L-fields, for instance, create, inform, and sustain literally everything in nature. Yet they are not a chemical process, not a mechanical sequence, not anything that pre-1960s scientific models ever described or even believed in. L-fields, say those who study them, literally sculpt us and all life-forms, yet they're not "literal" at all. They're intangible. To even explain how they're detected requires a treatise more reminiscent of St. Thomas Aquinas than Sir Isaac Newton.

Moving further into the transrational: morphogenetic fields are called metafields for the same reason metaphysics is called metaphysics. These fields are "above" (meta) the material realm, and can be neither seen nor measured. Indeed, in the words of scientist Rupert Sheldrake, they are "free of matter and energy" entirely! Yet morphogenetic fields, Sheldrake and others say, "shape and direct the entire animate and inanimate creation." When, for instance, a cut sprig of willow is jammed into the ground and watered, it is matterless, energyless morphogenetic forces from outside the matter and energy of the sprig that cause an entire tree to grow from the cutting. Likewise, when a dragonfly egg is tied off in the middle, unseen fields from outside the egg cause an entire insect to grow from each of the two halves.

We have in my view entered another True Wilderness. Though we're still studying science, we now stand amid energyless, matterless, invisible powers that "shape and direct the entire animate and inanimate creation," and these powers are no more graspable than the contents of those Hubble-glimpsed galaxies eleven billion light-years away. I'm not trying to deify morphogenetic fields here. What interests me is the fact that I'm speaking of things beyond my comprehension—but beyond science's comprehension as well. There is something poignant in this to me. Imaginative writers and contemplatives are used to the company of things beyond comprehension. Some scientists are not. Is there anything we more experienced Uncomprehenders can do to help these scientists feel more comfortable with swimming in the end where you never touch bottom?

That all things are shaped by fields that are beyond energy and matter is now what we must oxymoronically yet truthfully call "solid science." As a result, in the realm of language the scientific facts of our physical situation are becoming impossible to express in spiritually neutral terms. Science has moved in a generation from the easily stated but mistaken claim that we are mortal matter, chemical compounds, and little more, to the inspiring but linguistically problematic claim that we are living repositories of the invisible wisdom of primordial electromagnetic and morphogenetic fields. Scientists who disdain religion seem horrified by the mounting pressure to deploy overtly spiritual terms such as Jager, Teilhard, and Schumacher use. But the use of such terms does not mean you've turned into a fundamentalist trying to cure AIDS with Leviticus 14.

And what of science's own pet terms? It is probably less defensible, empirically speaking, to believe in a universe created by the Big Bang than in one created by Shiva's lingam.

"The Big Bang was not big, it was sub-atomic," writes Sara Maitland. "And it was not a bang, it was necessarily silent, since in the absence of time and atmosphere there was nothing to convey sound waves, and nothing to receive them either." I've read definitions of quarks, muons, and subatomic waves that sound less grounded than definitions of the Holy Ghost. My advice to scientists with regard to all this is: relax. If unseen fields beyond literary or scientific expression lie at the root of all life-forms and matter—if these fields are invisible yet deducible, ineffable yet artful, evasive yet omnipresent, and if in the attempt to describe them science has never sounded so much like ancient myth or scripture—so be it. I realize that to many an old school scientist the words "ancient myth and scripture" translate to "superstitious pap." But isn't this mere arrogance? Ancient thought as expressed in Wisdom literature is unanswerably profound and poetic, and scientists who study the ancients know this. Cutting-edge physicists have been pondering India's five-thousand-year-old *Upanishads* for decades, stunned by its exacting observations of how unseen fields and mayavic forces create this world of forms.

If it is ancient poetry that physics and fields are showing us, it's time that all good scientists opened their minds to poetry. If our problems cannot be solved at the same level of consciousness that created them, it's time we contemplatives, scientists, writers, artists, teachers, activists, and earth lovers transcend petty discomfiture, acclimatize to a more intuitive way of sensing things, and bring a reverence for the Unseen to bear on how we behave toward the seen.

Einstein: *In the new physics, there is no place for both field and matter, because field is the only reality.*

Willigis Jager: *There aren't two kinds of laws: matter and mind. Rather, there is a single continuous law for both matter and mind. Matter is the domain of space in which the field is extremely dense.*

Teilhard: *Concretely speaking, there is no matter and spirit. There exists only matter that is becoming spirit.*

Frederick Sommer: *Spirit is the behavior of matter. Perception does not take spiritedness into a state of affairs that does not already have it.*

Plotinus: *Let the body think of the spirit as streaming, pouring, rushing and shining into it from all sides.*

Stephen Hawking: *What is it that breathes fire into the equations and makes a universe for them to describe?*

John of the Cross: *The fire! The fire inside!*

Krishna in the *Bhagavad Gita: Behind the manifest and unmanifest there is an Existence that is eternal and changeless. . . . Having been, it will never not be; unborn, enduring, constant, primordial, it is not killed when the body is killed. . . . Weapons do not cut it, fire does not burn it, waters do not wet it, wind does not wither it.*

Living science.

IMPROVISATION #6: BEYOND-LANGUAGE

The word "mysticism" was unknown to me as a boy. My child mind excelled at acceptance, declined categorization, embraced spirit, matter, and contradictions without judgment, and everything that happened simply was.

The word "mysticism" still means little to me as an experiencer, since everything I experience continues to simply be what it is. But as the beneficiary of certain inner experiences that have guided my life, and as a writer in love with a world in which much of what is visible is abused and much of what is life-giving is unseen, my respect for the word "mysticism" grows if only because, by definition, it shepherds us toward realms in which "what is" is much more than physical. I am therefore stepping, this fine March day in my fiftieth year, out of a closet in which I've spent my writing life happily hidden, and openly confessing myself (with a blue-collar, rednecked blush) to be the experiential mystic I have, in fact, always been.

My lifelong love of rivers is partly responsible. In visiting the same streams year in and year out as Earth tilts on her axis, causing foliage, insects, fish, birds, seasons to arrive out of seeming nowhere, things occasionally tilt on some kind of interior axis, causing invisible yet artful, imperceptible yet detectable forces to arrive out of nowhere inside me. I have mostly used fiction as a repository for these unexpected falls into inwardness. But as I grow older I notice the way great nature-probing nonfictioneers from Blake and Wordsworth to Thoreau, Dickenson, Whitman, Muir, Jeffers, Merton, Gary Snyder, Wendell Berry, Pattiann Rogers, Mary Oliver, Jane Hirshfield, and on and on, unapologetically leap now and then in their writing, as they leap in their lives, from discursive language and the outer world into "beyond-language" and inner realms.

My friendships with a few people on this list, and my own life, have together convinced me: these linguistic leaps are based on simple fidelity to experience. When experience flies into realms that language cannot touch, honesty demands beyond-language.

Consider Henry David Thoreau. In a letter to one H.G.O. Blake, Thoreau unapologetically avers that humans can participate in the same kind of creative acts as the Creator Himself: "Free in this world as the birds in the air, disengaged from every kind of chains, those who practice the yoga gather in Brahma the certain fruits of their works. The yogi, absorbed in contemplation, contributes in his degree to creation. He breathes a divine perfume, he hears wonderful things. Divine forms traverse him without tearing him, and united to the nature which is proper to him, he goes, he acts as animating original matter. . . . Depend upon it that, rude and careless as I am, I would fain practice the yoga faithfully."

I have no rational idea what Henry is saying here. But I am struck by this:

Thoreau: *Divine forms traverse him without tearing him.*

Teilhard: *The divine assails us, penetrates us, molds us.*

What sort of experiences create such similar sentences?

Though famed for an astute Midwestern groundedness, Aldo Leopold too leapt, now and then, from natural history into mystical testimony. In *Round River*, for instance, he writes: "The song of a river ordinarily means the tune that waters play on rock, root and rapid. This song of the waters is audible to every ear, but there is other music in these hills, by no means audible to all. To hear even a few notes of it you must first live here for a long time, and you must know the speech of hills and rivers. Then on a still night, when the campfire is low and the Pleiades have climbed over rimrocks, sit quietly and listen for a wolf to howl, and think hard of everything you have seen and tried to understand. Then you may hear it—a vast, pulsing harmony—its score inscribed on a thousand hills, its notes the lives and deaths of plants and animals, its rhythms spanning the seconds and the centuries."

Reason protests such assertions. "A thousand hills!" it huffs. "Is this *science*? Is Aldo's *vast harmony* supposed to be audible? Then why can't I hear it? How can he claim to have heard something that spans centuries when he himself died in less than a century? This is a buncha late-night campfire woowoo. His editors should've cut it."

Reason makes all such leaps sound foolish, because they are foolish—to unadorned reason. But from boyhood through manhood it has been my experience that trying to grasp an insight, a deep mystery, a transrational experience, or any act of love via reason alone is rather like trying to play a guitar with one's buttocks. Our powers of reason, like our buttocks, are an invaluable tool. But not for the purpose of hearing "vast pulsing harmonies." As E. F. Schumacher put it, "Nothing can be perceived without an appropriate organ of perception."

This is not to demean reason. It's only to say that, unless trained like a bird dog to heel in the presence of love and mystery, reason lunges forth barking and snuffling, scaring off meta-meanings that only the heart could have hoped to embrace. When a superb reasoner like Teilhard says that "the divine assails us, penetrates us, and molds us," he has not left his sanity behind: only his reason. He is exposing matter to spirit. He's using beyond-language to do it. We can go with him. Our reason can't. The notion that we can stand apart from all things, infer the existence and true properties of all things, and solve the dire problems we've created for ourselves, with reason alone, is what I would call "Rationalist Woowoo."

In the medieval contemplative classic, *The Cloud of Unknowing*, the anonymous author states that "no evil can touch, and *no reasoning make an impact upon*, the divine creativity that proceeds from the depths of the soul." Spiritually speaking, nothing's changed since those words were set down. And the same words can be said of the symphony of forces woven through galaxies, unseen fields, synapses, ecosystems, subatomic particles, and cells. The physical universe, as we now understand it, cannot be accurately described via static or boxed-in modes of thought, for that which enlivens all things is dynamic, imperceptible, limitless, and—I believe with all the science of my heart— holy. We are steeped in and assailed by this holiness even as we study it. We have no objective distance from it and never shall.

IMPROVISATION #7:
MUSIC OF THE SPHERES

Another Teilhard declaration cited by Annie Dillard: *"It is precisely because he is so infinitely profound and punctiform that God is infinitely near."*

The first time I read this sentence I had no idea what it meant, so I looked up the word punctiform. Seldom has a dictionary had a more powerful effect one me: the instant I read that punctiform means "of the nature of a point or dot," Teilhard's sentence smote me with yearning. I still understood nothing, but my intuition sensed something incredible. Tying my reason by its leash to a figurative tree, I crept up on possible meta-meanings without it.

Pondering Teilhard's sentence in *For the Time Being*, Annie Dillard asks, "Is it useful to think of God as punctiform?" Her question sounded so odd and rhetorical that I expected a joke to follow. When instead Annie wrote, "I think so," I was suddenly covered with goose bumps.

Next Annie cited a scientific study on sand, of all things—informing us that the oldest grains of sand on Earth are the most perfectly spherical, and that a river takes a million years to move a spheroid grain a mere hundred miles.

Back at the tree, my reason howled, "What's any of that got to do with anything? These supposed observers of Earth are no longer *on* Earth! They're lost in space! And now you've tied me to a fuckin' tree and are wandering off with *them!* Come back! You *need* me!"

I answered my poor panicked doubting organ in this way: "Sit. Stay. I know I need you—to do stuff like my taxes. But there's something singing inside me, and I want to hear it, and your assertions bury the music. So take a rest. I'll be back in a while—hopefully."

My reason sank into a sulk. The rest of me sank into reflection:

The references to "punctiformity," to "the nature of a point or dot," to "nearness," all smote me with yearning. So did Annie's sentence: *The oldest grains of sand on Earth are the most perfectly spherical.* Why did she "answer" Teilhard with such a crazy fact? Why did that fact sing inside me?

Sitting quiet amid these questions—not trying to answer them, just enjoying their odd company—I suddenly fell through a floor inside myself and landed amidst an intensely recollected experience. To speak of it is to speak of a mystery intelligible to me only as mystery. I have no language with which to approach such an experience except beyond-language. I know before writing it that my description will leave me sounding like a fool to my reason. But I'm not getting any younger. The thought of dying without having described this wonder makes me feel like an ingrate. I prefer fools to ingrates, and try to live, act, and write accordingly.

I am far from alone. In the thirteenth century, Jalal al-Din Rumi spoke a spontaneous poem in Persian, which poem a disciple set down, scholars later translated into English, and the American poet Coleman Barks recently reconstructed to sound like this:

> *Don't go to sleep one night.*
> *What you most want will*

come to you then. Warmed
by a sun inside, you'll see
wonders. Tonight, don't put
your head down. Be tough,
and strength will come.
That which adoration adores
appears at night.

Beginning in boyhood but lasting well into manhood, I had a recurring experience, always at night, of what Aldo Leopold might call a vast, pulsing harmony and Teilhard an infinite punctiformity. Beginning when I was about twelve—always after long, vigorous outdoor days—I'd lie down in the dark, so dazzled by the wonders of the day that I would consciously swear off sleep in order to keep pondering all I'd seen and done.

While conducting these reviews I eventually entered a state wherein my body felt as though it was buzzing, and my eyes saw vividly in a waking dark. What normally followed this state was a clean fall into dream and sleep. My boyhood trick, though, was to fiercely resist that falling, and to keep gazing at whatever the night and my state let me see. I would "be tough." And sure enough, strength would come.

The beyond-language experience began when the vibration of my body was joined by an exquisite sense of density: of massive physical weight. This weight felt both vastly greater and vastly other than that of my body: a physical visitation by something heavy and huge, something a physicist might wish to call "a field." The only reason the weight didn't crush me, it seemed, was that it permeated me the way colors permeate vision or water permeates a sponge: I grew so absorbed that there was no "me" left to crush.

Shortly after the density grew palpable I heard an oceanic

hum: a single note, majestically deep and simple. To hear this note annihilated desire. The sound was so beautiful it was impossible to want to hear more. Any question I might have asked about who made it, where it came from, how it was produced, felt answered without speaking by the music itself.

Simultaneous to the sound, I saw, as plainly as I'd seen the light and objects of the day, an enormous sphere. This sphere, I knew instantly, was the source of the music, the density, and the massive weight. It floated in a sea of black. I hovered before it, its motionless satellite—though once the experience began, pronouns became impossible: "I" was now an invisible perceiver consisting of the senses of feeling, hearing, and sight. Body and mind were gone—and "I" was doing just fine without them.

The enormous sphere was beautiful to see, to hear, and to feel—a swirling mass of reds and oranges, lit from within, vast as a close-up star, though not at all hot. My being pulsed in tune with its massive hum, a sensation indescribably blissful, yet peaceful. Fear and excitement were not possible in this musical state. I had no ego to get excited with, no body to be afraid for. The sphere was not just the largest thing in existence, it was the *only* thing in existence, and I watched, felt, heard it in a state I can only call *adoration*.

But the experience grew richer. Every time I beheld the sphere the encounter had movements, like a symphony. Every time, the movements were the same:

First Movement: After "I" adored the sphere for a time, "I" would move toward it, and anticipation would fill me. My effaced self eased closer to the sphere till its dimensions seemed impossibly vast, its note capable of singing a universe into existence. Despite this potency, the sphere was all-gentle. The intimacy between us, when I could approach no closer, was as delicate as when we touch, with a cautious fingertip, the surface tension of still water. "I" remained on one side of this tension. *Infinitely profound and punctiform, infinitely near*, the sphere's music, light, and power reigned on the other.

Second Movement: When proximity to the sphere could not be closer, my point of view suddenly turned inside-out. I felt this hugely—a thrill something like when a jet plane hits an air pocket and drops a thousand feet, only not frightening. Once this inside-outing occurred I found that I could see, feel, and hear in the opposite direction. What I beheld brought bliss:

A second sphere had been born. The very twin of the first. Precisely as magnificent. Precisely as vast and profoundly close. The beautiful hum had also doubled. The discovery of the second sphere sent cataclysms of pleasure through me. (I'm trying hard to avoid sexual terms here.) An orb so vast it seemed all-encompassing had divided like a cell, creating a second all-encompassingness. Lodged between them, I turned one way, then the other, adoring them both.

Third Movement: Anticipation rose again. I withdrew slightly from the vast spheres in order to see them without shifting perspective. Then, as I watched/felt/listened, they divided like cells again, this time visibly, giving me a double "inside-out" feeling, creating four of themselves, their oceanic music a fourfold harmony now.

The plot thickened, grew fruitful, multiplied. The spheres created 8 of themselves, then 16, then 32, 64, 128, every orb glowing, lit from within, the music, bliss, sense of density and mass coming in waves, a vast, pulsing harmony. They loved to divide; loved to be fruitful. At each division I felt their love as if it were my own. Awash in this geometrical, musical mode, I watched the spheres go on dividing, grow incalculable in number, pour forth color, hum their multitudinous song, till they were so numerous I had to draw away in order to behold them all. Still dividing, still self-generating, they came to look like a vast wall of spheroid fruits, growing smaller with each division—first melons, then grapefruits, then oranges, apricots, wrong-colored grapes, then blueberries, then currants, then tiny seeds, till they became something too small for fruition—say, a vast field of singing, internally-lit grains of sand. (*"The oldest grains of sand on Earth are the most perfectly spherical."*)

Final Movement: The multitude of orbs kept halving till they became so minuscule that they could no longer remain separate: they divided into an infinity of grains so minuscule that they merged back into a single vast unity, their countless minute harmonies, too, joining in a single basso profundo note, till I realized that,

Da capo: I was back in the Beginning, gazing at the smooth, infinitely punctiform surface of the Original Vast Sphere. It floated in a sea of black. I hovered before it, a motionless satellite, in a state I can only call *adoration*. And the entire "symphony" commenced movement by movement, exactly as before, till I fell asleep in an exhaustion of density, division, creation, music, union, and bliss.

IMPROVISATION #8: FRUITS

There it is: a mystery intelligible to me only as mystery. I don't know beans about the "meaning" or "utility" of this experience. Such experiences don't care if they're comprehensible, useful, apropos, politic, polite: such experiences *assail*. But I've always loved and trusted the line: *By their fruits ye shall know them.* And in applying it to the spheres I realize that, mysterious as they remain, they have created tangible fruit.

When, for instance, I first heard of medieval cosmologists referring to a "music of the spheres," my faithful dog Reason howled, but the heart of me thought, *Why not?* When I read the Vedic description of a state in which the soul perceives infinite hugeness and infinite smallness as one and the same, and later came across the Koranic statement, *"All Creation in the hands of the Merciful One is smaller than a mustard seed,"* I both thought and felt, *Of course.* And when I learned of the mathematician Georg Cantor proving that infinities come in an infinite range of sizes, and read Paul Davies's discussion of Cantor ("Any [Infinity], being a unity and hence complete within itself, must include itself.... If it is One, then it is a member of itself and thus can only be known through a flash of mystical vision"), I thought, *Beautiful Spheres, Final Movement.* When I opened the dusty *National Geographic* this morning and saw galaxies swirling in a jot of universe "the size of a grain of sand held at arm's length," and when Teilhard's words then flipped these galaxies into my interior, my eyes filled because, for a timeless moment, I heard the profundo hum of a glorious old nighttime companion. And when I dreamed the other night that I was shot dead by a hundred machine guns, shot so many times that a dark bullet-driven wind blew my soul irrevocably away from my dead body and I was invisible and afraid and had neither breath nor voice with which to call out to my God, I called out in bodiless desire anyway, and a spheric and punctiform point pierced the grim world in which I drifted, the point expanded, tore that gray world's wall apart like so much wet tissue, a light poured through, and I saw my Beloved's cheek and brilliant eye peeking at me through the hole, just that much of Him, yet there was such love in that eye, such *What-a-trick-I've-pulled!* glee, that a posthumous existence without need of this body felt not just possible but certain, and I woke with a jolt of joy. And when, looking for Teilhard's "assailed" sentence this morning, I reread Annie writing *"There is no less holiness at this time—as you are reading this—than there was the day the Red Sea parted. . . . There is no whit less might in heaven or on earth than there was the day Jesus said, "Maid, arise" to the centurion's daughter, or the day Peter walked on water, or the night Mohammed flew to heaven on a horse. . . . In any instant you may avail yourself of the power to love your enemies; to accept failure, slander, or the grief of loss; or to endure torture. . . . 'Each and every day the Divine Voice issues from Sinai,' says the Talmud. Of eternal fulfillment, Tillich said, 'If it is not seen in the present, it cannot be seen at all' "* I felt nothing but an urge to shout: Go Annie! You're singin' the morphogenetic gospel now!

The sensations of weight, of palpable presence, of hum, still come over me now and again walking in cities and mountains, wading through traffic or trout streams. I don't consciously seek such sensations, they just check in, now and then, in the course of what comes. A spring aspen leaf might brush my face, and I close my eyes and find myself feeling the tiny, self-contained universe that is a spring-green aspen cell suddenly making two of itself, and thus growing, *because it loves to.* I witness "fruitful multiplication" in our Montana-winter-blighted fruit trees or the year's brood of bantam chicks, the creeks' insects or river bottoms' whitetail fawns, the newborn wood ducks, kingfishers, killdeers, and wonder comes upon me as the densities, unions, and divisions of love grow palpable. I've stood by the ocean, seen the subtle curve of horizon, felt the ocean's hum, and seen the seas as a single sphere. I've had the sense, standing in running water, that I've been not just close to the molecules flowing round me but inside them; that I've experienced, in the womb or aeons earlier, the coming together and breaking apart of spheric particles of H_2 and of O. I've witnessed plants, animals, family, friends migrating to known places or transmigrating to unknown; felt us jolt into new awareness or out of old bodies; witnessed our slow, sure breakdown by organic or industrial attrition, and our sudden, equally sure transformations of matter into soul when the thousand hills feelings and vast pulsing harmonies assail us with joy.

It's time I stopped building sentences now and stepped down to the creek, as I've done half my life, come evening. This time of year I'll look for the rainbows that migrate up from the bigger rivers to spawn. And I'll find a pair, if this spring is like the last eight, in a tiny side channel a quarter mile downstream. As I approach them on my belly I'll be crawling across spheroid grains of white granitic sand. I'll then bow like a Muslim to watch a female trout, an arm's length from my eyes, beat her body against gold-colored pebbles, build a stone nest, and fill it with a thousand lit-from-within orange spheres. I'll watch the male ease over like one of the gray-black snow clouds above. And when the milt pours down, each nested sphere will suddenly love to divide and divide till it's a sphere no longer, but a tiny, sphere-eyed trout. I'll encounter the same trout over the slow course of summer, drifting down toward the rivers, growing by dividing, defeating time; I'll catch them now and then, release most, eat a few to make miracle a part of me, and the survivors will return in twelve or sixteen seasons, bearing the milt clouds, glowing spheres, and hidden fields that carry the genius of trout toward my children's children's world.

There's not much more to discuss here. Either I'm crazy or I'm not, and the kingdom of heaven is within us or it isn't, and a divine punctiformity exists or it doesn't, and we sense it or we don't. If we do, God help us. And if we don't, God help us. Because if inner kingdoms and morphogenetic truth are delusions, where's the harm? You think Congress isn't deluded? If the punctiform spheres I've glimpsed are mere delusions, then Congress, the spheres, and I are three phantasms amid a chaos of delusions and one phantasm is pretty much as good as another, so hey ho, let's sally forth in the most gynormous internally-combusting phantasm possible and purchase only the choicest consumer delusions till the galaxies abort us, amen.

But if the punctiformities I've glimpsed in some sense *do* exist—if each and every day the Divine Voice *does* issue from Sinai, and if every inch of Creation is pierced by Its song and every dot, point, cell, particle, field is so moved by the Music that it loves to sing, swell, shrink, leap, divide, transform, and bear all fruit and all life and all death and all regeneration in response, well then *ahhhhhhh!* How grateful I am to be here! And how carefully and attentively I want to live!

I still have no rational idea what it means when consciousness revs up and perceives mystery amid mind, amid life, amid matter. But oh do I have images of what it means! I can't lend rational credence to Annie's sense that punctiformity is "helpful in sensing God." But I can lend a bit of beyond-credence. If we are ever to rise to new levels of consciousness or to the Beauty that is Truth, we've got to describe our perceptions as consciousness truly perceives them. I therefore confess my lifelong love for a wilderness found outside myself, till once in a while I encounter it within. It's a wilderness entered, it seems, through agendaless alertness at work, rest, or play in the presence of language, rivers, mountains, music, plants, creatures, rocks, moon, sun, dust, pollen grains, dots, spheres, galaxies, grains of sand, stars, every sort of athletic ball, cells, DNA, molecules, atomic particles, and immaterial forces. It's a wilderness that occasionally "inside-outs" me, leading to a Teilhardinian burning and Leopoldian harmony that leave my mind wondrous happy but far, far behind. It's a wilderness my trusty dog, Reason, will never succeed in sniffing out or chomping up, yet a wilderness I've been so long and gratefully assailed by that I've lost all but comic interest in the dog's endless hounding and suspect that even he begins to enjoy himself when the wilderness flips us inside itself.

I believe—based on phallic clouds giving birth to stars, spring stormclouds to snow, summer snowbanks to rivers, and orange orbs to trout; I believe based on punctiform dots melting into vastest spheres, spheres dividing their way back into dots, lives collapsing into ashes and dust, and dust bursting back to life; I believe based on spheric shapes singing, dividing, creating cells, plants, creatures, creating my children, sunflowers, sun, self, universe, by constantly sacrificing all that they are in order to be reconfigured and reborn forever and ever—that when we feel Love's density, see its colors, feel its pulse, it's time to quit reasoning and cry: "My God! Thanks!"

If I stake my life on one field, one wild force, one sentence issuing from Sinai it is this one: *There is no goal beyond love.*

＊ ＊ ＊ ＊ ＊ ＊ ＊ ＊

Acknowledgments

The many Christians still listening to their hearts despite waves of politicized, manufactured rote-think are a major inspiration for this book. So are the many remarkable "recovering fundies," jack-Mormons, and ex-Catholics I meet in my teaching and traveling.

The book's catalyst was Susan O'Connor. Its midwife was Laurie Lane-Zucker. Its nurse is Hob Osterlund. Its doctor is Phil Gardner. Its Irish first cousin and co-laugher- &-player is Brian Doyle. Among its editors, the most indispensible were Emerson Blake, Jennifer Sahn, Tracy Stone-Manning, Amanda Elkin, and Bill Thomas. Its agentry was done with the usual aplomb by the esteemed Michael Snell. Its Luddite author was saved from sixteen types of computer disaster by Mark Ratledge. The conqueror of my fear of cameras was Yogesh Simpson.

For shared stories, steady integrity, faith, and friendship that contributed directly to this book I thank my mother DJD the Elder, my wife Adrian, my children Celia, Ellie, and Tom, my Trappist brother Casey Bailey, the photographer and great teacher Emmet Gowin, the master flyrod makers Glenn Brackett and Rob Gorman, Craig Oberg and the Utah Academy of Sciences, Arts, & Letters, and my sisters and brothers of the pen and heart, Melissa Madenski, Dana Louis, Karlene Arguinchona, Gerri Haynes, Jessie Harriman, Jane Hirshfield, Judith Ernst, Melissa Bixler, Annie Dillard, Diane Tomhave, Sherman Alexie, OE's Sam Alvord and Doug Frank, Ian Boyden, Chris Dombrowski, Markar, John Bussanich, John Bateman, Tom Crawford, my nephews Casey and Andrew, and He whose Name, closeted though I keep it, has become inseparable from my ability to breathe.

Publisher's Acknowledgments

The Triad Institute would like to recognize Christina Lane; Susan O'Connor and the Charles Engelhard Foundation; Paula & Jeremy Sager, Bob & Marilyn Clements, Jeff & Nancy Clements, and the Clements Foundation; Tom & Sonya Campion; Laurie Rahr; and Tom & Lynn Meredith for their kindness and generosity to this project.

About the Author

David James Duncan is the author of the novels *The River Why* and *The Brothers K*, the story and memoir collection, *River Teeth*, the nonfiction celebration of Western rivers, *My Story as Told by Water*, and many stories and essays. His work has won a Lannan Fellowship, the 2001 Western States Book Award for Nonfiction, a National Book Award nomination, two PNBA Awards, an honorary doctorate from the University of Portland, the American Library Association's 2003 Award (with Wendell Berry) for the Preservation of Intellectual Freedom, inclusion in four volumes of *Best American Spiritual Writing*, and many other honors. David has spoken all over the U.S. on wilderness and rivers, literary and imaginative freedom, the irreplaceable importance of wild salmon, the pathos of fly-fishing, and on the writing life, the nonmonastic contemplative life, and the nonreligious literature of faith. He is a contributing editor to *Orion*. He scripted and narrated an award-winning 2005 documentary on the natural history of bamboo flyrods titled *Trout Grass* (see <troutgrass.com>), and is doing the same for *The Fire in Water*, a film on the unnatural history of the Interior West's vanishing wild salmon. David lives, writes, and "home-churches" in western Montana.

THE
TRIAD
INSTITUTE

Laurie Lane-Zucker, the cofounder and former executive director of The Orion Society, founded the Triad Institute in early 2005. Triad is a nonprofit organization devoted to developing and advancing a new vision of citizenship that is simultaneously local or "place-based," national, and multinational/global. Triad serves as a think tank, publisher, and education organization. *God Laughs & Plays* is Triad's first book.

For more information on Triad's programs

www.triadinstitute.org

Triad Institute, Inc.
P.O. Box 601
Great Barrington, MA 01230
info@triadinstitute.org

BOARD OF DIRECTORS
Laurie Lane-Zucker, President & CEO
John Elder
Guido Rahr III, Treasurer

BOARD OF ADVISORS

Kenny Ausubel	Van Jones
Jacques Baudot	Cheryl King Fischer
Mark Dowie	Robert McDermott
David James Duncan	Bill McKibben
Peter Forbes	William H. Meadows
Benjamin C. Fortna	David Orr
Paul Hawken	Alec Webb
James Hillman	Tu Weiming
Pramila Jayapal	Terry Tempest Williams